# The Great American Divide

How we got here and what we can do about it

## D. Robert Pike Ph. D

# DEDICATION

To Terri Trester

May God be with you and strengthen you
in this hour of trial.

===============

In memory of my precious little Fifi.

# CONTENTS

# ACKNOWLEDGMENTS

I acknowledge our founding fathers who by the grace of God were empowered to create the best national document the world has ever known:

## The Constitution of the United States of America.

I also wish to thank my friend and fellow Author Ron Workman who proofread this book for me, and helped straighten me out on a few punctuation items I have been getting wrong. Ron also writes some terrific novels for Christians. I have often told him that his novels would make excellent Hallmark movies.

And of course, I wish to thank my precious wife Ida for putting up with me and being a continual source of inspiration for me.

# Foreword

It's funny how people's lives often intermix. I vividly remember my and my wife's first encounter with Rob and his wife Ida. Marjorie, my wife, and I had just moved to Greenville, South Carolina, and put a contract on a new home which was under construction. One Saturday we were at the home thinking about paint colors and carpet choices when Rob and Ida walked in. They were also house-hunting and seemed disappointed when we told them that "this is our house." We chatted a few minutes and they left – strangers, in and out of our life in only a few minutes, we thought.

The next day, Sunday, we visited a local church which was near the home. Guess who else was visiting the same church that Sunday. You guessed it, Rob and Ida. That was almost nineteen years ago, and our friendship is still growing. Rob has been my Sunday school teacher, confidant, and seemingly always there if my family needed him. God has been keeping us together, I believe, because we need each other's love and support. We both have homes in Indiana and, until recently, both had homes in North Port, Florida. At one time he and Ida were living in Georgia, just 40 miles from where Marjorie and I lived in Alabama. What I am trying to say is that I know this man. He is a man of God and daily seeks God's will for his life.

*The Great American Divide* is Rob's fourth book. His first three were more on Biblical doctrine but, in my opinion, a prerequisite for *The Great American Divide*. What Rob has accomplished in this book is to bring many of our current political thoughts to the table for discussion. I couldn't stop reading. He has expertly explained the "how we got here" of many of our current failures as a nation. Did you ever wonder what it means to be a conservative or a liberal? What about the good and/or bad of each? Rob explains this in a way that "makes sense." He talks about racism, slavery, and fascism in their role in our nation's history. He talks about God and makes a strong challenge to anyone claiming to be an atheist.

He presents all of the above to make us think about our nation and its relationship to our God, not the Islamic God which has no place in the culture of our United States of America. He explains the historical damage our nation has suffered and continues to suffers because of our nation's leftist movement away from the God of our fathers.

I am proud to write this foreword for *The Great American Divide* and recommend it to everyone, conservative or liberal. History doesn't lie; it gives those who will listen and learn from its mistakes a second chance to make corrections. Then, for the things that were "done right," it gives us the opportunity to build upon our successes. I believe our forefathers "got it right" when they constructed our Constitution. I see no reason we as a nation would want to stray away from this great document.

We have a new president, Donald Trump, who also believes in our constitution. Let's all support him in his efforts to "Make America Great Again." Whether you are left-wing or right-wing in your thinking, we all love our country. Not supporting our President is a losing scenario for all of us.

I am also a writer, but I write fiction. My stories do carry a moral theme, but, in the end, they are fiction. We live in a "real world." Things that happen in our world are real and have "real" consequences. As you read Rob's book, please remember that he is talking about things and events that, if not checked, can destroy our nation. Please, let's not allow these things to happen.

As a footnote, I would love for you to take a look at any or all of my novels. You can find them on Amazon under author, Ron Workman. May God bless and keep you.

Ron Workman, MBA and Author

# Prologue:

# A Changing Nation

The date is Saturday, July 20, 1957. I had just turned 10 years old. Our family was somewhat poor and there was not very much frivolity in our household. Our nation was living in a time of relative peace. Dwight D. Eisenhower was in the second term of his presidency, and the worst threat we had present with us as a nation was the threat of nuclear war with the Soviet Union. But Eisenhower kept the pressure on the Russians, and the threat appeared to most people to be minimal. The space race had not begun, although the Russians would launch Sputnik in the coming months. Sputnik was the first artificial satellite to orbit the earth. It was small, only about 2 feet in diameter, and contained an internal transmitter with four antennae which transmitted signals in the 20 MHZ and 40 MHZ radio bands. During its short time of three moths in orbit, it proved to be very successful in broadcasting radio signals, proving the value of having orbiting satellites to aid communication. This also led to the creation of NASA in this country.

At 9:30PM my dad popped a couple of bowls of popcorn and rationed out Coca Cola to me and my two brothers. We had already settled down in our modest abode of a home to enjoy our favorite Saturday night lineup on TV. This included **Perry Mason** on at 7:00PM, followed by the **Perry Como** show. With our popcorn, we watched our two favorite Westerns, **Have Gun will Travel,** and **Gunsmoke**. Amazingly, there was not a single utterance of a "cuss" word on any of these TV programs, or any of the only 3 TV networks in existence, ABC, CBS, and NBC. This carried over into the lives of everyone. If any of us boys uttered such words in the presence of our Dad or our Mom, we knew what was coming. We would get our butts whipped. My Dad's choice was a belt, and my mother used a wooden spoon. But these threats kept us in line and did not hurt us.

This is because we were truly living in a nation where Judeo Christian values were solidly in place.

We knew that the Bible taught that it was good to spank children. Look it up yourself. (Proverbs 13:24; 22:15; 23:13,14; just to name a few) Now we are living in a time where we have seen mothers who spank their children in public being threatened to have their children taken away from them! What is the result of this? It seems that we see far too many children that seem to be **the ones in control**. They have taken over the role of "boss" in the family. Whereas the parents seem to be lost, not knowing what they can do to bring their bratty kids under control. Something is really wrong here. Yes, it gets back to basics. The Word of God has the answer....spank those little brats! It will not hurt them!

Life in that time was so much different from now that it is almost like we are living on a different planet. Looking back on that time, I believe it is correct to say that life was much simpler. The threats to the United States were very conventional threats, but, at least, we knew who our enemy was. There were some people who were afraid enough of the Soviet Union's nuclear threat to build fallout shelters but this was very rare. Although the "Cold War" was going on in political circles, there was very little said about it anywhere except in the news. The word "terrorism" was not in our vocabulary. There was no cable TV, therefore there were no "News" channels, **many**

**of which** today do not give **ANY** real news at all, only left-wing propaganda which puts on a façade of being news. Contrast all of this with 60 years ago. It was absolutely forbidden that anyone should use foul language on TV of any kind.

The TV news was for the most part considered to be extremely reliable, as personified in news anchors such as Edward R. Murrow and his successor Walter Cronkite, who was once proclaimed as the most trusted name in journalism. This was a time in our history where America was a haven of conservative values. This was personified in many ways. Even the TV Series "Superman" expounded in its opening the values of "truth, justice, and the American way."

People who wanted to immigrate here came legally because they truly wanted to live as Americans do, work hard, enjoy the fruits of their efforts, and learn the language, the culture, and enjoy the freedoms that Americans enjoyed. Those who immigrated had to work hard to become Americans. This gave them an overwhelming sense of pride. It instilled in them a strong sense of nationalism, and a strong sense of wanting to preserve the values of our nation.

Contrast that with the myriads of illegal immigrants who have invaded our country who have no desire to adapt to our culture. Cheered on by the left-wing media and liberals, they come here to change our country, and in many places they have made huge areas of this country just like the hell hole they came from with one big difference. Here they have the freedom to desecrate our flag, our nations Judeo-Christian values, our language, and our way of life. They are taking all the handouts allowed by the left wing radicals who have been running this nation in recent years, and believe that they are even entitled to more.

As I write this section we are in the early days of the Donald J. Trump presidential administration. Instead of praising our new president for his hard work ethic, the left-wing radical media is doing everything they can to destroy his presidency. Driven by the radical liberal ideologist billionaires, they are paying protesters to come in and create anarchy wherever possible.

Why they are doing this is truly mind boggling. Those of us who still claim to be conservatives are praising God that Hillary Clinton did not win the election, thus promoting more of the same for another four to eight years.

Stepping back again 60 years, and,,, having lived through it all, we see radical changes everywhere. In the music world, the most radical change at that time was probably in 1956 when Elvis Presley stepped onto the stage of the Ed Sullivan Show. He soon became extremely popular. It didn't take long for him to be the King of Rock and Roll. And although his appearance was controversial at the time, it was nothing compared to what we see in many of the Rock bands for the past thirty years or so. Now we see everything from being just short of complete nudity to explicit sexual mimicking on the stage. Extremes in costume and look are so common in the music world now that just about anything visual that musicians do in public is written off as being normal in the music industry.

So how did everything change so much in the short time of just 60 years? What has made our society so different than it was back then? We have "In God we Trust" on all of our money, but do we trust in God? We have a war going on in this country between conservatism and liberalism. How do we know which is right? We see constant partisan bickering in our federal government that makes it almost impossible to get things done; Why?

What part has been attributed to our lack of spiritual values as they have been driven throughout these past six decades? What can we do about it now?

These are all questions we will be facing in this book as we go forward. May God help us as we strive to stem the tide of a destructive wave that has encompassed our nation.

# In God we Trust – Really?

**Is this moto still true?
Can we trust our educational institutions to teach these principles?**

The Lord Jesus said: "The Spirit of the Lord *is* upon me, because he hath anointed me to preach the gospel to the poor; he hath sent me to heal the brokenhearted, to preach deliverance to the captives, and recovering of sight to the blind, **to set at liberty** them that are bruised," Luke 4:18 (KJV)

The Apostle Paul said: "Now the Lord is the Spirit; and where the Spirit of the Lord is, **there is liberty**." (2 Cor 3:17) NKJV

If we look back on our history, the motto, **"In God We Trust"** was adopted by the United States in

1956. It was then added to our United States paper currency, replacing the original Latin motto which was "E pluribus Unum," meaning "out of many – one." That term goes all the way back to the beginning of our nation, and was adopted when the Seal of the United States was created and adopted in 1782. One of the passages that has been noted as the basis of the motto is Psalm 118:8 which says: "It is better to take refuge in the LORD than to trust in man."

Although the phrase has been on our coins for much longer, the term "In God we Trust" has been on our paper currency since I was a 10 year old child, having been approved by the 84th Congress of the United States, and signed into law by President Eisenhower in 1957. On the fiftieth anniversary of the motto, it is interesting that Congress passed a resolution to reaffirm the motto. Considering that there has been so much opposition to this phrase, that may be surprising to many of us. But it did have overwhelming support and passed by a vote of 396-9. This should help us to believe that this is something that God wants us to have as a motto! After all, if you believe in the absolute sovereignty of God, we know that what God wants, He always gets.

It is amazing that it is still on our currency as I write these pages. It is comforting to me to pick up a brand new coin and see this inscription on it. But keeping this has not been without a fight as many secularists and atheists have sought vigorously to have that motto eradicated from everything we know and love in this country.

In an article entitled: **In God We Trust: America's Historic Sites Reveal Her Christian Foundations** By Stephen McDowell, he points out that this and many other scriptural references also appear in many of the most important public buildings in our nation's capital. These passages and mottos have been built into many of these structures in such a way that it would be very difficult to remove them. He notes that this is unique among the history of the world. But a historic tour of our nation makes it clear that our founding fathers birthed our nation on a firm reliance on Almighty God and his Son Jesus Christ.

In this article, McDowell points out that the list of buildings in the nation's capital that have memorabilia and inscriptions indicating a strong faith in God, These include:1[1]

The Library of Congress
The Supreme Court
The Capital Building
The National Archives
The Washington Monument
The Lincoln Memorial
The Jefferson Memorial
The White House

Each one of these has its own story. I have included a summary of several of these, taken from Stephen McDowell's research as shown below:

## The Supreme Court

The Biblical foundation of American law is evidenced throughout this building. On the outside East Pediment is a marble relief of Moses holding tablets containing the Ten Commandments. Engraved on the oak doors at the entrance of the Court Chamber are the Roman numerals I through X, and above the

---

[1] http://providencefoundation.com/?page_id=1962 ; Many Thanks to Stephen McDowell for this information concerning the inscriptions on buildings in the nation's capital.

heads of the Justices is a carved marble relief with a large stone tablet containing I through X in between two allegorical figures, representing The Power of Government and The Majesty of the Law (each set of numerals represents ancient law, that is the 10 commandments). In the main foyer are marble busts of previous Chief Justices, many of whom were Christians such as John Jay, the first Chief Justice, and John Marshall, the most prominent in the early years. Each day the Court is in session, a crier ends his call announcing the formal opening by declaring, "God save the United States and the Honorable Court."

## The Capitol Building

All of the eight large paintings in the Rotunda present aspects of our Christian history. A few include: The Landing of Columbus — Columbus said he was convinced to sail because "it was the Lord who put into my mind" and that "the Gospel must still be preached to so many lands." The Baptism of Pocahontas — This shows the baptism of one of the first converts in the

Virginia colony . The Virginia charter said they came to propagate the "Christian Religion to such People, as yet live in Darkness and miserable Ignorance of the true knowledge and worship of God." Departure of the Pilgrims from Holland — shows the Pilgrims observing a day of prayer and fasting. William Brewster is holding an open Bible upon which is written: "The New Testament of our Lord and Savior Jesus Christ." "God With Us" is written on the ship's sail.

Also in the Rotunda are carved reliefs including: Penn's Treaty with the Indians — Penn called his colony "a holy experiment" and said of it that "my God that has given it to me . . . will, I believe, bless and make it the seed of a nation." The Landing of the Pilgrims — "having undertaken for the Glory of God and advancement of the Christian faith."

In God We Trust, our national motto, is inscribed in letters of gold behind the Speaker's rostrum in the House Chamber. Also in this chamber, above the central Gallery door, is a marble relief of Moses, the greatest of 23 noted law-givers (and the only one full-faced). In 1867 the House Chamber was the meeting place for the largest Church congregation in America. This was not unusual for Churches had been meeting in the Capitol from its beginning.

Statues of many early leaders are displayed throughout the Capitol. Most of these people were Christians (and many were ministers), including George Washington, James Garfield, Samuel Adams, Rev. Peter Muhlenberg, Rev. Roger Williams, Rev. Marcus Whitman, Daniel Webster, Lew Wallace, Rev. Jason Lee, John Winthrop, Rev. Jonathan Trumbull, Roger Sherman, and Francis Willard. Many plaques in the Capitol declare our faith as well, including: In God We Trust, placed above the Senate main door; "What hath God Wrought!" — the first message sent over the telegraph in 1844, found on the Samuel F.B. Morse Plaque outside old Supreme Court Chamber.

The Prayer Room contains an open Bible sitting on an altar in front of a stained window showing Washington in earnest prayer. Behind him is etched the first verse of Psalm 16, "Preserve me, O God, for in Thee do I put my trust."

## The Washington Monument

From the tallest structure in Washington a message of Praise be to God goes forth. Engraved upon the aluminum capstone on the top of this 555 foot monument is Laus Deo. Inside the structure are carved tribute blocks with many Godly messages: "Holiness to the Lord," "Search the Scriptures," "The memory of the just is blessed," "May Heaven to this union continue its beneficence," In God We Trust," "Train up a child in the way he should go, and when he is old, he will not depart from it."

## The White House

An inscription by the first President to inhabit the White House, John Adams, is cut into the marble facing of the State Dining Room fireplace. It reads: "I pray Heaven to Bestow the Best of Blessings on THIS HOUSE and on All that shall hereafter Inhabit it. May none but Honest and Wise Men ever rule under this Roof." Each President has attended church, associated with the Christian faith, taken the oath of office with their hand on a Bible, and referred to God in their inaugural addresses.

## The Lincoln Memorial

The words engraved upon the walls of the Lincoln Memorial reflect the Christian faith and providential perspective of our 16th President, Abraham Lincoln. On the south wall is the Gettysburg Address which ends exclaiming "that this nation, under God, shall have a new birth of freedom — and that government of the people, by the people, and for the people, shall not perish from the earth." On the wall of the north chamber is Lincoln's Second Inaugural Address which shows his knowledge of the Scriptures: "Both read the same Bible and pray to the same God, and each invokes His aid against the other. It may seem strange that any men should dare to ask a just God's assistance in wringing their bread from the sweat of other men's faces, but let us judge not, that we be not judged. The prayers of both could not be answered. That of neither has been answered fully. The Almighty has His own purposes. "Woe unto the world because of offenses; for it must needs be that offenses come, but woe to that man by whom the offense cometh" (Matthew 18:7)."

As I conclude this quotation from Stephen McDowell's article, I would like to note the final quote he stated as taken from the 1854 U.S. House of Representatives:

"The great vital element in our system is the belief of our people in the pure doctrines and divine truths of the gospel of Jesus Christ." We as a nation must not forget that God is the author of our liberty, for if we do we shall lose it.

So with all of this background, wouldn't you think we are living in a nation that is totally Christian? Wouldn't you think that it would be reflected in the actions of those in power as well as those who are dwelling in this land of liberty?

As I mentioned earlier, the term "In God we Trust" has been on our paper currency since having been approved by the 84th Congress of the United States, and signed into law by President Eisenhower in 1957. On the fiftieth anniversary of the motto, it is interesting that Congress passed a resolution to reaffirm the motto. Considering that there has been so much opposition to this phrase, that may be surprising to many of us. But it did have overwhelming support and passed by a vote of 396-9.

But is this truly what is in the heart of most Americans? Let's look into this. First of all, I would like to say that I believe that there are **very few** true Atheists in America. The old saying that "there are no atheists in the foxholes" is true. When people are confronted in a life threatening situation, almost everyone will appeal to God, even if there has been no evidence of faith throughout their entire life. Furthermore of those claiming to be atheists, I think that they cannot truly be atheists, but are at most agnostics. Let's look at definitions of these terms.

1. Atheism - disbelief or lack of belief in the existence of God or gods.
2. Agnosticism - a belief that nothing is known or can be known of the existence or nature of God or of anything beyond that which exists as material phenomena; a person who claims neither faith nor disbelief in God.

Do you see the subtle difference here? I believe that it is nearly impossible for anyone to say with **absolute certainty** that they do not believe in the existence of God. If they truly examine the evidence, there is just too much evidence to the contrary. Thus, I would say that if someone makes that claim, they are not being honest.

## A quick study in Apologetics

How do we know that the Bible is a reliable guide for our lives? One quick way to prove this is because of the fact that it contains many fulfilled prophecies concerning Jesus the Messiah. Why do we say that this is proof positive? Have you ever made predictions about anything? How accurate were your predictions? Even if you had advance knowledge that would help you, chances are your rate of accuracy would most likely have been very small. Now, what happens if these predictions contain a lot of detail? Yes! That would increase the likeliness that you would be wrong. But the Bible contains prophecies which have proven to be extremely accurate.

A few examples should suffice:

The prophet Daniel predicted that **exactly 483 years** after the decree to rebuild the city of Jerusalem and the temple, the Messiah would appear on the scene.

> Daniel 9:25 "Know therefore and understand, *That* from the going forth of the command To restore and build Jerusalem Until Messiah the Prince, *There shall be* seven weeks and sixty-two weeks;

23

This order went forth to build the wall in 457 BC. Jesus appeared as the Messiah when he began his ministry in AD 27. The prophecy came true **to the exact year.**[2]

The prophet Micah predicted the **exact city** of the birth of the Messiah **700 years** before it happened.

> Micah 5:2  "But you, Bethlehem Ephrathah, *Though* you are little among the thousands of Judah, *Yet* out of you shall come forth to Me The One to be Ruler in Israel, Whose goings forth *are* from of old, From everlasting."

Yes, this was written 700 years before Jesus was born in Bethlehem. It came true exactly as prophesied.

The **exact method** by which Jesus was to be executed (death on the cross) where his hands and feet would be pierced was not even thought of when it was predicted in Psalm 22. It was also predicted that **he would be thirsty**, that **they would divide his garments** among them, and that people would be staring at him.  Here we see:

---

[2] For more information see my book, **God's Promise of Redemption, a story of fulfilled prophecy,** 2015 Truth in Living Publishing p.82

I am poured out like water, And all My bones are out of joint; My heart is like wax; It has melted within Me. My strength is dried up like a potsherd, And My tongue clings to My jaws; You have brought Me to the dust of death. For dogs have surrounded Me; The congregation of the wicked has enclosed Me. They pierced My hands and My feet; I can count all My bones. They look *and* stare at Me. They divide My garments among them, And for My clothing they cast lots. Psalm 22: 14-18

These things came true exactly as prophesied, and recorded in the Gospel Accounts of Jesus.

In fact there were 48 prophecies about Jesus in the Bible which He fulfilled. Why would God give such a great number of prophecies concerning the presence of the Messiah on the earth? The answer should be obvious. By doing so, **it would make it impossible** for there to be **an imposter** to be fulfilling this role.

When I was in college, it was necessary for me to study statistics. A good statistical analysis is the engineers friend and was a part of my job while I was working in industry. So let's look at the probabilities here. What are the probabilities of one man being able to fulfill all of these prophecies? As you will now see, this number would be too large to calculate.

In his book, **The Case for Christ**, Lee Strobel points out just how impossible it would be for anyone to "accidently" fulfill these prophecies. Professor Emeritus of Science at Westmont College, Peter Stoner, has calculated the probability of one man fulfilling the major prophecies made concerning the Messiah. Notice what he found out:

> Stoner also computed the probability of fulfilling forty-eight prophecies was one chance in a trillion, trillion, trillion, trillion, trillion, trillion, trillion, trillion, trillion, trillion, trillion, trillion, trillion, trillion, trillion, trillion.[3]

In numeric value this is $1,000,000,000,000^{15}$. There is not even any way for the human mind to begin to calculate a number this big. In fact as Strobel points out this number is so big that it represents a number equal to the number of atoms

---

[3] See **The Case for Christ, A journalists Personal Investigation for the Evidence for Jesus,** Paperback edition, 1998 Zondervan, p. 247

in a trillion, trillion, trillion, trillion, billion universes the size of ours.

Yet despite these startling statistics, Jesus himself was the man who fulfilled all of these prophecies. Are you surprised about all of this? This is the basis of our faith! It is just as the passage says:

> Mark 10:27  But Jesus looked at them and said, "With men *it is* impossible, but not with God; for with God **all things** are possible."

## Our Disgraceful Educators

When the most prestigious Universities in the country were founded, almost without exception, they were founded as Bible believing Christian Institutions. This includes Harvard University, The College of William and Mary, Yale University, and Princeton University.

Harvard University, which was founded in 1636 in Cambridge, Massachusetts, was one of these. One of the ways a student from Harvard would be labeled as "fit" to have a degree was by showing that they could read from the Old and New Testaments of the Bible in the Latin language and show that they understood what they were reading. Yale University also began in the 17th century. It was founded by ten clergymen all of whom graduated from Harvard. Its original purpose was to train future ministers of the faith.

The College of William and Mary was established in the British Colony of Virginia in 1693 as a college of Divinity, Philosophy, and Languages. A little over 50 years later the College of New Jersey was formed. It was founded by the Presbyterians, and was later renamed as Princeton University. Its original purpose was to train ministers of the New Light Presbyterian faith.

Today these Universities are dominated by liberals whose thought is not at all in keeping with their original charter. In fact they are now almost exclusively institutions of liberal thought.

Today many millions of dollars are paid out to educate the youth in the 21$^{st}$ Century. The values which permeated these oldest institutions are long gone. The professors in these institutions are wielding an enormous amount of influence over the young and impressionable minds of our youth. Even though the majority of Americans today still identify with the Christian faith, we find that the values of the Christian faith are totally underrepresented in our nation's institutions of higher learning. What are our beloved youth being taught today? Are they even teaching our beloved that there is a God? What kind of "truth" is being taught in these institutions?

A study was done by the Barna Group in 2015.[4] The results are very interesting.

> This group combined atheists and agnostics into one group, which they called *skeptics*. Skeptics were then defined as people who either do not believe God exists at all or are not sure God exists. What they found was that skeptics represent one-quarter of all unchurched adults (25%). They further found that Nearly one-third of skeptics have never attended a Christian church service in their lives (31%), which is nearly double the proportion of those unchurched people who are *not* skeptics (17%).

> This study also found out that skeptics are younger, more educated, and contain more women than 20 years ago. They also found that they are more ethnically diverse, and more regionally diverse than 20 years ago.

---

[4]https://www.barna.com/research/2015-state-of-atheism-in-america/

Why is this so? What is it that has propelled our society more toward skepticism concerning the nature and belief in the existence of deity? Barna also noted that there were three primary reasons:

1. Rejection of the Bible as God's Word
2. Lack of trust in the Churches of Christendom
3. Continued cultural reinforcement of the secular worldview

Yes, they believed that the Bible was simply a book of well-known stories or that it is a historical document. In both cases, they did not believe that it had Divine guidance in its production. In fact, those students who claim to be Christian today in our American colleges are ridiculed and subject to a great deal of discrimination. These institutions do this while at the same time declaring themselves to be devoted to tolerance and diversity. But they will be much more tolerant and less discriminatory of anyone whose religion is not Christian.

But regardless of all of these facts and the outcome of this investigation, Barna noted that 6 out of 10 of those skeptics have at least one copy of the Bible in their possession, and a few still read it occasionally.

When we look at the reasons mentioned above for such a lack of faith, mostly among young people, we must look deeper into the reasons. If we dig into the background of this we have to realize that since most skeptics are more educated than ever before, it **must** have to do with **the way they are educated.**

The colleges in America are more liberal than ever before. They are now the single most liberal entity that is influencing our young people. Note what was discovered by Tim Groseclose in this study:

According to a study by professors at Smith College, George Mason University and the University of Toronto (they surveyed 1,643 full-time faculty at 183 four-year schools), 72 percent of professors at American universities labeled themselves liberal, while just 15 percent said they are conservative. 50 percent of faculty members identified themselves as Democrats and only 11 percent Republicans.

Political Science professors Robert Lichter of George Mason University, Neil Nevitte of the University of Toronto and Stanley Rothman of Smith College also found that 51 percent of those surveyed said they rarely or never attend church or synagogue. Neil Nevitte of the University of Toronto and Stanley Rothman of Smith College also found that 51 percent of those surveyed said they rarely or never attend church or synagogue.

These liberal leanings translate into liberal political beliefs. 84 percent of those surveyed are strongly or somewhat in favor of abortion rights, 67 percent think homosexuality is acceptable, 88 percent want more environmental protection "even if it raises prices or costs jobs" and 65 percent want the government to ensure full employment, which puts the professors to the left of the Democratic Party.

Later on in this same study we find:

A quick Google search of "liberalism on college campuses" brings a wealth of good evidence that what is being taught on many of them is anti-American, anti-religious, anti-Israel, pro-gay rights and pro-abortion, often to the exclusion and ridicule of opposing views.

In December, Columbia University appointed a committee to look into charges of bias and intimidation by faculty, particularly in Middle East studies. Columbia isn't the only university with bias problems when it comes to the Middle East. Checkout www.campus-watch.org for many more examples.

Ward Churchill, a tenured professor at the University of Colorado, is in the news for his grotesque characterization of the 9/11 victims as "little Eichmanns" who were not casualties of terrorism, but legitimate "military targets." His views are part of his teaching.

From "gay rights" courses, even majors, at an increasing number of colleges, to the usual anti-military and anti-free enterprise bilge that has been documented in numerous books and articles, only those who are in complete denial would claim there is no link between the mostly liberal views of professors and how they shape their subject matter in the classroom, at numerous forums and in campus advocacy groups that constitute modern academic life.

Thomas Reeves of the Wisconsin Policy Research Institute has said "conservatives are discriminated against routinely and deliberately" in faculty hiring, making some highly qualified teachers virtually unemployable because of their political and social views. This guarantees a perpetuation of a one-dimensional approach to most subjects.

In matters of race and gender, colleges practice affirmative action to employ more minority and female professors and attract more students with these characteristics. Why won't they do the same for conservative professors and students in the name of diversity, pluralism and academic freedom?[5]

In his book, "Left Turn," Tim Groseclose noted:

Economists Christopher Cardiff and Daniel Klein have conducted an extensive examination of the political beliefs of university professors. They found that, in general, Democratic professors outnumber Republican professors by a 5: 1 ratio. However, this varies considerably by field. For instance, in sociology the ratio is 44: 1; in ethnic studies, 16: 1; political science 6.5: 1; physics 4.2: 1; economics, 2.8: 1; electrical

---

[5] http://www.campus-watch.org/article/id/1809

[6] Groseclose PhD, Tim. Left Turn: How Liberal Media Bias Distorts the American Mind (Kindle Locations 2428-2431). St. Martin's Press. Kindle Edition. From Christopher F. Cardiff and Daniel B. Klein, "Faculty Partisan Affiliations in All Disciplines: A Voter-Registration Study," Critical Review 17, nos. 3– 4, (2005): 237– 55.

engineering 2.5: 1; accounting, 1.2: 1; and finance, 0.5: 1.1[6]

But even with all of this, wouldn't you think that these universities would be protectors of the freedoms that allowed them to sway so far from their original underpinnings and be guardians of academic freedom? This is obviously not the case. These classrooms are for the most part under the control of a liberal dictator whose desire it is to create more graduates that are like him. This means that if a student is a Christian, his views will be subject to an incredible amount of bigotry and discrimination. The dominance of the theory of evolution is a prime example. Many of these liberal professors will fail a student if their class papers include anything which alludes to Biblical creation instead of the more acceptable Darwinism that they espouse.

In his book "Persecution" Author David Limbaugh wrote a chapter entitled "The Battle for the Academy." In this chapter, Limbaugh shows several examples of Universities who like to proclaim tolerance for all, while at the same time being totally intolerant of Christians. This intolerance is noted in many areas of college life, from the hiring practices which exclude Christians, to the scholarships that have been withdrawn from students once it was discovered that the student was a Christian. Christian Professors are losing their positions or being demoted at a rapid pace because of the practice of religious discrimination against Christians in word and in deed.

One such example of such a lack of tolerance comes from a college near where I grew up in Indiana. It involves Professor Janis Price who had been teaching there for fifteen years. She was charged with creating a hostile environment at DePauw University in Greencastle, Indiana. What was her "sin?" Notice what Limbaugh reported:

> She placed issues of Dr. James Dobson's magazine *Teachers in Focus* on a table in the back of her classroom. She advised students that the publication contained articles written from the Christian viewpoint, which they could peruse if they chose to, but they would not be required to, nor would any assignments be made concerning them.

> An article in one of the magazines addressing how the teachers should approach the issue of homosexuality in public schools offended a student who made the decision to complain to the administration. Vice President of Academic Affairs Neal Abraham sent

Professor Price a letter of reprimand accusing her of providing students of "intolerant" material, which "served to create a hostile environment in violation of school policy. Abraham went so far as to characterize Price's actions as "reprehensible." He backed up his words by cutting her salary by twenty-five percent and suspending her from her teaching responsibilities. Abraham's explanation? "The university cannot tolerate the intolerable."[7]

I'll bet that if there was a magazine with an article in it about the merits of Sharia Law in the Muslim Community, not a word would have been said to this professor. In fact Limbaugh reported in his book that a colleague of the professor who received the reprimand stated that it is required of all professors to be tolerant and politically correct in all other areas except when it comes to Christianity... all of this despite the fact that DePauw University has Methodist underpinnings. That is why I have repeatedly stated that even

---

[7] Limbaugh David, Persecution, How Liberals are Waging War Against Christianity p. 118. Taken from Andrea Garrett, "Intolerant Intolerance: Anti-Christian Bigotry on Campus" CBN-News.com, July 10, 2002

parents who send their High School graduate teens to a "Christian" College, it is still necessary to be diligent in checking out what they are learning while there.

## The 2016 Student movement towards Socialism

Leading up to the Presidential election of 2016, a proclaimed socialist candidate, Bernie Sanders, a Senator from Vermont ran against Hillary Clinton. It was amazing the amount of support that came from college students all across America. In fact, to counter this, Hillary Clinton moved even further left in order to garner some of that support away from Sanders. But if the students truly understood their history about socialism in the early days of this country, would this even have been an option for them? Had they studied their history of the Pilgrims, this is what they would have learned:

## Socialism and the Pilgrims

A group of Pilgrims came to America in 1620, convinced that since they were all devout Christians, a purely socialistic society would work for them. Although they were two centuries earlier than Karl Marx, their social experiment was based on the same premise. That premise was:

"**From each** according to his ability, to each according to his needs"

The experiment was set up on a purely social hypothesis. Prior to leaving from Plymouth England in 1620, they all signed a contract. According to its provisions, each of the participants were required to pool all of their profits they got from the work they did into a common pool, no matter what their profession, no matter how hard they worked, or what they did. They were to take nothing out for themselves from their efforts, but **they would only take** from the common stock of goods what they needed to live. **So how did this social experiment work out for them?** Note what William Bradford, the colony's first Governor wrote about this:

> The first two years the result was shortages and starvation. About **half the colonists died**. **No one did more than the minimal** because the incentive to excel was destroyed. The industrious were neutralized. Bradford wrote of the scarcity of food "no supply was heard of, neither knew they when they might expect any." The socialist experiment Bradford added, "was found to breed much confusion and discontent and retard much employment that would have been to the benefit and comfort. For the

young men, that were most able and fit for labour and service, did repine that they should spend their time and strength to work for other men's wives and children without any recompense...." **In other words, socialism made strong men lazy**. In another book written by the same author, *History of Plymouth Plantation*, Bradford spoke of another problem because of the government created famine—thievery. Even in this Christian community, "much was stolen both by night and day...."

After two years of such, with the survival of the colony at stake, they contemplated upon "how they might raise as much corn as they could, and obtain a better crop than they had done, that they might not still thus languish in misery." **They opted to abandon the incentive killing socialist contract in favor of the free market.** And so they "assigned to every family a parcel of land, according to the proportion of their number, for that end..."

The effects were almost immediate. A delighted Governor Bradford wrote: "This had very good success, for **it made all hands very industrious**, so as much more corn was planted than otherwise would have been by any means the Governor... could use, and saved him a great deal of trouble, and gave far better content. The women now went willingly into the field, and took their little ones with them to set corn; which before would allege weakness and inability; whom to have compelled would have been thought great tyranny and oppression." In other words, the free market is a much greater stimulus than governmental force. The Pilgrims now wished to work **because they got to keep the benefits of their labor.** "Instead of famine now God gave them plenty," Bradford wrote, "and the face of things was changed, to the rejoicing of the hearts of many, for which they blessed God.... Any general want or famine hath not been amongst them since to this day."[8]

Philosopher George Santayana wrote many years ago, "Those who cannot remember the past are condemned to repeat it." This makes me very fearful of what today's students have failed to learn. Do you really think that if our students were taught about this failed experiment in socialism that Bernie Sanders would have been such a

---

[8] Taken from an article written by Dr. Harold Pease at http://libertyunderfire.org/2011/11/1430/

popular candidate in the colleges of America during this election season? Do you really think that if the students understood the history of the failed countries that practice socialism, they would have supported a candidate like this? It shows that our institutions are failing to teach history to our students.

Can we help the fact that our universities are like this? Not at the point where we find out these atrocities. Is there anything we can do about it? YES! Who's fault is it that these kids are growing up as learned left leaning liberals. **It is the fault of the parents!** We as parents just assume that the Universities are going to teach our kids the truth, when actually they are just **propaganda mills for the left**. If more parents would stop their high school graduate children from going to these Universities because of issues like this, they would be forced to change their policies. We must face the fact that these kids are taught principles which are contrary to the Bible, and contrary to what most mainstream American households want their children to learn...including the sanctity of life. This includes teaching them that fetuses are nothing but a glob of protoplasm, unworthy of life until they are born naturally. This means that it is OK for them to be aborted all the way up to the time of birth.

How many of those kids being taught this nonsense would actually be horrified if they saw how a partial birth abortion was accomplished? What would they do if they saw the doctor who was performing the abortion take that precious baby out of the womb except for the head, and **poke a hole in the back of the head and suck the brains out.** Do you really think they would still believe that this was not murder?

And yes, those who continually preach against discrimination do discriminate themselves. They are directly taught to discriminate against conservatives. This crosses all racial, religious, and socioeconomic ties! It is absolute hypocrisy, but it is a fact.

I want to come back to what I said earlier. I said that the reason these kids are growing up with such distorted and ungodly views is the fault of the parents. King Solomon wrote this passage thousands of years ago, and it's never been more appropriate than it is now.

> Proverbs 22:6 "Train up a child in the way he should go, And when he is old he will not depart from it."

Do parents of children in the 21st Century truly take this passage seriously? What is the meaning of the phrase, "Train up a child." It implies much more than one might think. It suggests an **extremely important** call to activity. This means that parents are charged with the very important responsibility to actively commit their children to a specific course of action that would include **the proper training** about our Creator and the Biblical principles upon which our nation was founded. This does not mean that they should just randomly trust these institutions. It involves active participation, not passive reliance on the educational institutions of our day.

Does this mean that we as parents should do all of the training and education of our children ourselves? No, not necessarily. It does mean that we should be good stewards of the education of our children. We should know **exactly** what the core principles of what **any school** is teaching that is going to be entrusted with the minds of our children.

So now, what about those of us who have violated this rule, and have turned our children over to the masses to get an education? Are we shocked when our children come back with left-wing liberal thinking such as we have seen above?

Additionally, we must consider that our children are the most precious natural resource that we have. Are these children being trained in such a way as they can be useful in society? We need to inspire them to be aggressively pursuing an education that will benefit them in their chosen field, whether that be as manufacturing employees, skilled trades workers, educators, social workers, legislators, or physicians.

This is imperative in view of the fact that many of these kids just quit on their educations and drop out. When this happens, a tragedy of life is bound to occur. A high school dropout will earn considerably less than a high school graduate, will have worse health, and will die sooner than a graduate. For college dropouts they too earn far less and have fewer opportunities than college graduates. Let's be sure to keep these kids in school!

## Liberal Institutions produce Liberal graduates

The Leadership Institute was founded in 1979 and provides training in campaigns, fundraising, grassroots organizing, youth politics, and communications. The Institute exists to teach conservatives of all ages how to succeed in politics, government, and the media.

Here is what the Leadership Institute found out recently. In the following excerpt please note my source below[9]

America's college campuses have become cesspools of leftism. Here are just three recent stories the Leadership Institute has uncovered:

1.  Students at the University of Maryland, who pay up to a whopping $44,645 per year to attend, <u>couldn't identify Ronald Reagan after being shown a photo of him</u>.

2.  At the University of California-Irvine, their legislative council <u>voted to ban the American flag</u> in their student government lobby, calling it "a weapon of imperialism" that doesn't belong in an "inclusive space."

3.  A professor at Polk State College in Florida <u>gave a student four zeroes in a row on essays</u> – because she refused to write them in a way that would deny her Christian faith.

This is all thanks to leftist control of our nation's colleges. Leftists knew one of the best ways to undermine America was to raise up generation after generation of students ignorant of our country's rich, patriotic heritage.

But it goes beyond that.

**Not only do leftist professors leave out our country's rich heritage in their lectures, they indoctrinate students to hate America.**

Professors spew their venom at students day-in and day-out:

- America is evil.
- Old Glory is a symbol of genocide.
- The Founding Fathers were oppressors.
- Conservatives are racists.
- Communism is the cure for the world's ills.

Impressionable students – even those who grew up in conservative, patriotic homes – end up parroting the same garbage they hear in the classroom.

And if a conservative student tries to stand up for herself, like the one at Polk

State College who refused to deny her Christian faith in her essays, the professor fails that student – <u>sabotaging her grades and her future career</u>.[10]

We cannot leave this important topic unchecked. If we do, then conservatives may lose our colleges altogether … and then we lose our country.

Is this shocking for you to hear that such a thing is **firmly entrenched** in our institutions of higher learning? **It should absolutely be!** So what can you do about it?

Organizations such as **The Leadership Institute** or **Minding the Campus** may be helpful. I have investigated and found the following organizations can help in fighting this fully entrenched movement from the left.

These conservative organizations have been noted at the **Minding the Campus** website listed below:

1. <u>**The Intercollegiate Studies Institute**</u> inspires students to discover, embrace, and advance the principles and virtues that make America free and

---

[10] https://www.leadershipinstitute.org/crazycolleges/

prosperous. ISI-supported Reading Groups receive free books and help in bringing speakers to campus, while the Collegiate Network supports liberty-minded student newspapers and campus publications. The ISI Honors Program brings 50 undergraduates to an all-expenses-paid week-long conference and numerous colloquia, offers free books and resources, and pairs each Honors Fellow with an academic mentor. ISI also offers grants and fellowships to graduate students and sponsors essay contests.

2. **The Foundation for Economic Education**'s mission is to offer the most consistent case for the "first principles" of freedom: the sanctity of private property, individual liberty, the rule of law, the free market, and the moral superiority of individual choice and responsibility over coercion. FEE hosts seminars for both high-school and undergraduate students (most expenses paid), and FEE's online library provides video and audio lectures.

3. **The Institute for Humane Studies** seeks to advance liberty by supporting undergraduate and graduate students who are interested in individual freedom. While the institute is based at George

Mason University, registration is free and open to all students. Each year, IHS awards over $750,000 in scholarships, in addition to sponsoring seminars and fellowships for graduate students and outstanding juniors and seniors. With the Koch Foundation, IHS also offers paid internships in journalism and public policy.

4. **Hertog Political Studies Program**, held in D.C., is a six-week seminar investigating political theory and public policy, with a subsequent two-week fellowship that delves deeper into a particular topic. Each session is guided by an academic scholar or policy expert. Students receive a stipend to cover all expenses.

5. The **Publius Fellowship,** sponsored by the Claremont Institute for the Study of Statesmanship and Political Philosophy, is awarded yearly to college seniors, recent graduates, and graduate students pursuing careers in politics, scholarship, or journalism. For two weeks, Publius Fellows meet to read and discuss great works of political philosophy. The fellowship includes a stipend, travel expenses, and housing.

6. **FIRE** (the Foundation for Individual Rights in Education) seeks to defend and sustain individual rights at America's colleges and universities, including freedom of speech, legal equality, due process, religious liberty, and sanctity of conscience. FIRE works with college administrators to ensure that school policies protect and do not violate individual rights, using media campaigns and, when necessary, legal means. Through FIRE's website, students can submit reports on violations of individual freedom. [11]

If you have a student that is preparing to further his or her education, it would certainly **behoove you** to investigate these organizations to help prepare them for the onslaught of liberal thinking that is certain to follow in these colleges. Remember that it is **your responsibility** as a parent to be on top the details about the education that your child will be getting. This is covered in

---

[11]

http://www.mindingthecampus.org/2012/09/six_organizations_every_conser/

the biblical command given in the Old Testament book of Proverbs which is still very much appropriate today:

> **Proverbs 22:6** "Train up a child in the way he should go, And when he is old he will not depart from it."

> **Ephesians 6:4** Fathers, do not provoke your children to anger, but bring them up in the discipline and instruction of the Lord.

Note the words "**when he is old** he will not depart from it," and "bringing them up in the discipline and instruction of the Lord." While it is true that unless you will be sending them to a Christian College, it is very unlikely that they will get any Christian training, it is also true that **you must be careful** to at least have a plan in place to counteract all of the negative liberal training that may be present in most liberal educational institutions.

I would like to also add that if you are sending your kids to a Christian College, it **does not mean** that you can believe that there is **no danger** of liberalism being taught in these institutions. Remember the words of Jesus:

"At that time the disciples came to Jesus, saying, 'Who is the greatest in the kingdom of heaven?' And **calling to him a child**, he put him in the midst of them and said, "Truly, I say to you, unless you turn and become like children, you will never enter the kingdom of heaven. Whoever humbles himself like this child is the greatest in the kingdom of heaven. 'Whoever receives one such child in my name receives me, but whoever causes one of these little ones who believe in me to sin, **it would be better for him** to have a great millstone fastened around his neck and to be drowned in the depth of the sea.'" (Matt 18:1-6 ESV)

It is **your responsibility** as a parent to do your homework and make sure that your precious child does not have his mind hijacked by these purveyors of falsehoods. In God we trust means just that! No matter **what circumstance** we are in, we **PUT OUR TRUST IN GOD!**

President Ronald Reagan stated:

Our National Motto – 'In God We Trust' – was not chosen lightly. It reflects a basic recognition that there is a divine authority in the universe to which this nation owes homage.

To me, to repeat this phrase and truly mean it is something which is life-saving. It is the absolute essence of the life of the ages. In his writings in the New Testament of the Bible, the Apostle Paul said:

"The word is near you, in your mouth and in your heart" (that is, the word of faith that we proclaim); because, if you **confess** with your mouth **that Jesus is Lord** and **believe** in your heart that God raised him from the dead, **you will be saved**. For with the heart one believes and is justified, and with the mouth one confesses and is saved.

For the Scripture says, "Everyone who believes in him will not be put to shame." For there is no distinction between Jew and Greek; for the same Lord is Lord of all, bestowing his riches on all who call on him. For "everyone who calls on the name of the Lord will be saved." (Romans 10:8-11 ESV)

**"In God we Trust"** is a simple reiteration of what King Solomon stated years ago in one of the most **prosperous societies in the history of man** when he said:

My son, do not forget my teaching, but let your heart keep my commandments, for length of days and years of life and peace they will add to you. Let not steadfast love and faithfulness forsake you; bind them around your neck; write them on the tablet of your heart. So you will find favor and good success in the sight of God and man. **Trust in the LORD with all your heart,** and do not lean on your own understanding.

In all your ways acknowledge him, and he will make straight your paths. Be not wise in your own eyes; fear the LORD, and turn away from evil. It will be healing to your flesh and refreshment to your bones. Honor the LORD with your wealth and with the first fruits of all your produce; then your barns will be filled with plenty, and your vats will be bursting with wine. (Proverbs 3:1-10 ESV)

This was the message of the founding fathers, and **if we want to keep our republic** which was founded by these brave men. it will be our message too.

# What is Conservatism?

*We the People of the United States, in Order to form a more perfect Union, establish Justice, insure domestic Tranquility, provide for the common defence, promote the general Welfare, and secure the Blessings of Liberty to ourselves and our Posterity, do ordain and establish this Constitution for the United States of America*

*The Preamble to the Constitution of the United States of America - 1787*

The framers of the Constitution of the United States of America were men of diversity. When I say that, I mean diversity of thought, diversity of action, and diversity of socio-economic status. They were passionate men whose lives had been abused by the rule of British Authority. The political and philosophical differences between

Great Britain and the American Colonies had been brewing for quite some time and was about to explode.

Most likely, this explosion came in the form of the Boston Tea Party which occurred on December 16, 1773. It was an act of outrage on the part of a Patriot group known as *The Sons of Liberty*. They had made it their stated will that they would fight in earnest against the extreme taxation, and the complete violation of the rights of the colonists. As such, they destroyed a shipment of tea in Boston Harbor. The reasons for this were complicated. But it made a huge statement to the British Government that they would not let them try to monopolize the sale of tea through the East India Tea Company. The Sons of Liberty had already taken another grandiose stand against the British government with the opposition of the Stamp Act in 1765.

The British Government felt justified in issuing the Stamp Act to help finance the cost of their troops in the colonies. The way it worked was that all paper used for legal means as well as newspapers, magazines and other paper was to be supplied by the British Government and would be embossed with revenue stamps. This posed a horrible burden on the colonists, and thus the opposition by The Sons of Liberty.

This brought on even more extreme measures on the part of the British Government as they closed Boston Harbor and tried to execute a series of measures which they hoped would bring these rebellious colonists back in line. It could arguably be stated that the Boston Tea Party was the **actual beginning of the American Revolution** against Great Britain. Eventually, the colonists, realizing the severity of the situation got together and formed the First Continental Congress in which they would collaborate in their resistance. This was called in response to the punishment issued by the British government to the commonwealth of Massachusetts for the rebellion of the Boston Tea Party.

Actual combat broke out in 1775 when the British Government tried to seize the weapons of the colonists. (This later led to the second amendment) This resulted in the battles of Lexington and Concord, and the war was on. In response to this, the colonies called the Second Continental Congress. They appointed George Washington to take command of the newly formed Army and coordinate the militia. This was a **government of necessity**. It was not to be the final form of government for the 13 colonies.

On July 2, 1776, the Second Continental Congress formally voted to become independent of the

British Government and as such, it issued the Declaration of Independence on July 4, 1776.

## The American Revolution

It seems almost inconceivable that the colonies could possibly think that they could wage war against the British Government. The entire population of the colonies at the time was less than three million people including about a half million slaves. The population of Great Britain was about four times this. Add to this the fact that the Continental Congress which had been set up as the Governing body of the colonies was totally lacking in resources. There was no official government or any of the things which come with a government such as a legitimate colonial military, or a colonial governmental financial system. Instead what the colonists had was a sort of a rag-tag government which was operated by a group of true Patriots who called themselves forth from the thirteen colonies. These Patriots did have the advantage of being well educated, but they certainly were not elitists. But they were men who were willing **to sacrifice all** for the cause of Liberty. To add to the uncertainty of such a thing happening, this government was formed **after the war had already begun!**

The reason for their patriotism was stated in the preamble to the constitution which was written above. It was to form **a more perfect union**! They had already been working hard in their individual colonies, and liked the union that each of them had already formed through their individual states, but wanted to add the federal side merely to tie it all together and unify them to fight off the tyranny at the hands of the British. They had seen what it was to live under a more burdensome union, and they wanted a government that respected individual liberty. They had seen injustice to a heightened degree in the regulations and taxes imposed on them, and were living difficult lives due to the authoritarian rule of the British Government. As the preamble stated they did this for not only their own benefit, but for the benefit of their posterity. This means for future generations living in this government. We today are still the beneficiaries of their vision and patriotic love of their newly formed country.

You must realize that the framers of the constitution came together to form a federal government **out of necessity**. At the time of the forming of the First Continental Congress, the nation was **already in an undeclared war** with Great Britain as described earlier. It was necessary to form a federal government in order to give it broad powers that could not apply to the individual states. But for the most part, it was **never the intention** of the framers of the constitution to create a federal government to be **any larger than it had to be**. How do we know this? It is because they each had a vested interest in their **individual states** and how they would be affected. They did not want to grant any more broad powers than necessary to an entity which would effectively control these states!

Thus, they created a republic instead of a democracy. A republic would **give equality to each of the individual states,** and, in so doing it would automatically **limit the power of the federal government.** The framers were much more interested in their individual states and the laws that they had already created being maintained well past the necessity of the Continental Congress.

There are some who would try to tell you that the framers of the constitution were conservatives, but actually, the opposite is true. These men were idealists, perhaps they could even be labeled as radicals. There was nothing conservative about what they were doing. They were trying to take a relatively small army which they had formed and radically change the government of the colonies, and they succeeded in doing just that. The true conservatives at that time were those who wanted to preserve the bond with Great Britain. Although they may have disagreed with the tyranny that they were living under, they wanted to preserve the British way of life in the colonies.

So this begs the question: **What do you mean by conservatism?** Yes, this term needs to be defined. It may be defined many different ways. Some would say that they are conservatives because they want to preserve all of the radical changes that have been made in our way of life in the last fifty years. If this is their goal, and they truly want to preserve these degrading ideas, I guess you could say in some deranged sense of the word they have defined themselves correctly. So when speaking of conservatism, there is one very important fact that you must understand, and that is this: **True Conservatism does NOT have an underlying ideology.** Did you get that point? I would like to reiterate it. There is really no such thing as a conservative ideology. As I stated previously, the framers of the constitution were **NOT** conservatives. They were doing everything in their power to radically change the government. In that sense, we could call them **PROGRESSIVES!**

Conservatism means just what it says: A conservative is **one who conserves**. If you are a spendthrift, and you want our government to be the same way, then you are a fiscal conservative. If you were a hard core Communist in the old Soviet Union, and you were a conservative, then you would have wanted to preserve these ideals for posterity; that is for the future generations of Soviet youth. But Communism **IS** an ideology which is based in socialism. That is why it was called the Union of Soviet **Socialists** Republic. Its ideology was one of socialism. And as is often said of this ideology, it fails "when you run out of other people's money." This is exactly what happened that led to the demise of that government.

But this is not the definition of conservatism as it is known today in the United States. American Conservatism today is totally focused on the **keeping** of the Constitution, the Declaration of Independence, and the related documents intact while considering changes **only if absolutely necessary.** To Conservatives, it is to be preserved in order to protect the ideals projected in the preamble of the Constitution which I quoted at the beginning of this chapter. Since the Constitution is now constantly under attack, this is the biggest battle that conservatives face right now.

## The Constitution - a Document to be Preserved or Changed?

Now we have come to the point of discussing the biggest debate regarding the Constitution. Is this a document that is to be valid throughout the ages? Or is it a document that should be changed as the culture in America changes? This is the argument upon which we are about to embark.

You have undoubtedly heard the term Constitutional Conservative. In its purest form this is a person who believes that the Constitution should be preserved the way the framers intended it to be understood when it was written.

On the opposite end of the spectrum you have what is known as the Progressive movement. This originated in the Progressive Era, which began at the end of the 19th century and continued through the early part of the twentieth century. During this period of time, social reformers wanted to change things for the reason that they believed the Industrial Revolution ushered in a new system of thought appropriate for the time. This, along with much of the thought promulgated during the age of enlightenment, is what has formed the beginnings of liberalism as we know it today. For Progressives, freedom has a different definition than that of conservatives.

Conservatives believe what the original framers believed; that we have more liberty with a smaller government and less regulations. The Progressive Liberal believes that freedom is obtained when people fulfill their dreams through the expansion of government, and that the primary function of government is to help people fulfill their ultimate potential through regulation. Now I appeal to your senses here. Which one sounds more like freedom . . . more government with more bureaucracy and more regulations. . . or limited government with limited bureaucracy and limited regulations? With bigger government and more regulations, it goes without saying that this will **limit the liberty** of the people. This was actually the basis of the American Revolution . . . to get past all the tyrannical regulations, taxes and other burdens.

It seems very clear to me that if you empower government to tell you how you must live your life, you are in effect handcuffing yourself to the government. The end effect will always be tyranny.

## Constitutional Conservatism

Since the Constitution defines the government, the conservative view of the purpose of the constitution is to limit the federal government to exactly what is outlined in the document. In fact, I would say that this is at the core of conservative thought in America. As previously stated, the Constitution was written in such a way to limit the power of the Federal Government and keep as much power as possible in the individual states.

This means that **the framers** of the constitution wanted the federal government **to be small**.

President Ronald Reagan made it perfectly clear that this was his belief in his very first inaugural address in 1981:

"In this present crisis, government is **NOT** the solution to our problem; government **IS** the problem!"

But conservatism in America today is also much more than that. It involves the keeping of the things that made life simple in America decades ago. It involves giving people the freedom to make it on their own; to become everything they want to be. Conservatism does not like the idea of continually upping the debt through spending, and of giving out unnecessary handouts. Doing this restricts the strength, potential and creativity of the people, and makes them slaves to the state. One of the most **loved and hated** men in America is Rush Limbaugh. At a CPAC conference in 2009 here is what he said about Conservatism:

I want to tell you who conservatives are. We conservatives have not done a good enough job of laying out who we are because we make the mistake of assuming that people know. What they know **is largely incorrect** based on the way we are portrayed in pop culture, in the drive by media, by the democrat party. Let me tell you who we conservatives are: **We love people**. When we look out over the United States of America, when we are anywhere, when we see a group of people such as this or anywhere, we see Americans.

We don't see groups, we don't see victims; we don't see people we want to exploit. What we see is potential. We do not look out across the country and see the average American, the person who makes this country work. We do not see that person with contempt. We don't think that person doesn't have what it takes. We believe that person can be the best he or she wants to be if certain things are just removed from their path like onerous taxes regulations and too much government. (Thunderous applause delay)

We want every American to be the best he or she chooses to be. We recognize that we are all individuals. We love and revere our founding documents: The Constitution, and the Declaration of Independence. We believe that the preamble of the constitution contains an inarguable truth. That we are all endowed by our creator with certain unalienable rights, among them are life, liberty, freedom, and the pursuit of happiness. (Much more applause) Now those of you watching at home may wonder why this is being applauded. **We conservatives think all three are under assault.**[12]

What Limbaugh has stated here is correct. Perhaps it is not an all-encompassing definition, but it did give those watching this speech at CPAC a pretty good idea of what American conservatism means. **American Conservatives do love people**. We are not radical nutcases like the mainstream media and the Democrat party like to portray us. We want **ALL** people to reach their ultimate potential by allowing them the freedom to succeed. We do love the things that are espoused by the original document created by the second Continental Congress. Yes, what Rush was quoting was actually from the Declaration of Independence when it said:

> "We hold these truths to be self-evident, that all men are created equal, that they are endowed **by their Creator** with certain unalienable Rights; that among these are Life, Liberty and the pursuit of Happiness."

---

[12] https://www.youtube.com/watch?v=u0bTRdLmi7U

By espousing the beliefs of the Declaration of independence, the framers wanted a government "of the people, by the people, and for the people." This meant that the government was designed to **work for us**. We **do not** work for the government. It was to be a government where the leaders were selected by a democratic process in the States, but since each of the states wanted an equal say in the process of selecting a President and in representation in that government, it was a Republic on the federal level.

Those who wrote these original documents were indeed men of integrity. They were radical idealists, who wanted to abdicate the Throne of England; and yes **they believed in the fact that GOD endowed men with these rights** and made that very clear in the original documents.

### Conserving Judeo-Christian Values

When we define an American Conservative we also have to look at the **conservation of moral values**. The founders expressed what are commonly called Judeo-Christian values. This means the values that are expressed in the Old and New Testaments of the Bible. That is why American Conservatives were opposed to removing the teaching of The Ten Commandments given by Moses to the Israelites in the Bible book of Exodus, chapter 20. It is why we are opposed to the removal of prayer in the schools. That is why we hate it when the name of Jesus is degraded and not even allowed to be mentioned in public circles, while at the same time the names of Mohammed, Buddha, and Confucius, are not a problem.

Christian Conservatives want to conserve the values of Christianity as defined in the Bible, particularly those values espoused in the Gospels by Jesus. This is why Rush Limbaugh said what he said earlier. **American Conservatives love people**. We love them by wanting them to succeed on their own. We do not want them to live on the paltry handouts of welfare as promulgated by the Leftists. We want to help them in every area of their life to succeed. This means they are **free to fail.** But some will say: What do you mean? **Why would you want anyone to fail?**

It is because **failure is a critical component of success.** Conservatives do not believe in participation trophies. The **only** way to success is through failure. Thomas Edison is the purest example of this. He failed in the process of making the light bulb over a thousand times. But this is not how he viewed it. Instead, he viewed it as 1000 steps in order to achieve success. There are many examples of this. Let's consider a few.

Did you know that Abraham Lincoln failed also? He went to war as a Captain, and returned as a private. After leaving the military, he failed as a businessman. He was defeated many times in elections after he entered Politics but did not give up before eventually becoming President of the United States. The great automaker Henry Ford failed five times and went completely broke before finally succeeding. Babe Ruth was known as the home run king, but for a long time, he was known as the strikeout king, etc.

Most American Conservatives believe that **our rights come from God**, not the government. Thus we want to **conserve** the idea stated in the Declaration of Independence: "all men are created equal, that they are endowed **by their Creator** with certain unalienable rights." We want to **conserve** the idea that "among these are Life, Liberty and the pursuit of Happiness." We want to **conserve** freedom of religion as espoused by the founders. They risked everything to come to what they called "The New World" to be able to freely practice their religion, a religion based on these Judeo-Christian values. That is why most of the Ivy League Universities were originally set up, **YES** it is true, they were set up for the purpose of training ministers of the faith. Don't believe it? Check it out.

## Are these Values under Assault?

Rush Limbaugh stated at the end of the video, which I quoted above, that the values of liberty, freedom, and the pursuit of happiness under the banner of the original documents of this country are under assault. The reason he has stated this is as Conservatives, we believe in the philosophical principle that a life of liberty and freedom is a culture that must be preserved, and defended. So why is he saying this?

It is because what has emerged in the 21$^{st}$ century is the emergence of a worn out philosophy based on the values of socialism. This is now used by those educated in our institutions of higher learning that is openly hostile to the values that we hold so dear. These are people who are puffed up with their own elitist brand of "knowledge." They have been persuaded by the adoption of similar philosophy as that of our former President to believe that the values we hold so dear from our founders are flawed; that the best way to preserve freedom is through larger government.

President Obama believed that we built our society on the principles of Colonialism. Accordingly, it seems to be his belief that we stole the land from the native people before us, and built our nation through injustice. He touted that this nation was built on the backs of slaves who were treated unfairly by the colonialism of Great Britain, and that as a result of this, we don't deserve anything that has been achieved in this country.

That is why we have seen so much from former President Obama in the way of his well-known apology tours he undertook during his presidency. But under President Obama, who in my opinion is a radical Progressive, every value that we hold dear is under assault. These values which the Progressive movement are pushing are the same values that history shows has destroyed many powerful nations in our past. In the Introduction to his book *Ameritopia: The Unmaking of America* conservative author Mark Levin has this to say:

> The symptoms of tyranny that threatens liberty and republicanism have been acknowledged throughout time, including iconic Americans. For example, Supreme Court associate justice Joseph Story, among America's most prominent legal thinkers, explained in 1829,

> "... governments are not always overthrown by direct and open assaults. They are not always battered down by the arms of conquerors, or the successful daring of

usurpers. There is often concealed the dry rot, which eats into the vitals, when all is fair and stately on the outside. And to republics this has been the more common fatal disease. The continual drippings of corruption may wear away the solid rock, when the tempest has failed to overturn it. . ."[13]

We know this to be true. Great civilizations have rotted from the inside out, primarily because of the degradation of moral values. This was especially true in the Roman Empire. The main cause of their decline was the destructive immoral behavior exhibited in the elite circles of their society. The immoral behavior overtook their leaders to the point of ruining the entire society. As associate justice Joseph Story pointed out, "the continual drippings of corruption" eventually wore away their solid rock when this corruption was allowed to continue. **Now I must ask you the question:**

**Does the following sound familiar?**

---

[13] Levin, Mark *Ameritopia: The Unmaking of America,* 2012 Threshold Editions A division of Simon and Schuster Inc. p. ix, x Levin was quoting from *"The Value and importance of Legal Studies"* The Miscellaneous Writings of Joseph Story, ed. (Boston: Little, Brown, 1852), 513

When Barrack Obama was elected in 2008, he was determined to change America. He said over and over again "Change has come to America." **We had no idea how right he was.** He was intent on changing America **fundamentally**. Much of his Anti-colonialist philosophy is outlined in his book: "Dreams From my Father." As such it was his view that the more affluent countries of the world such as The United States of America are living a better life right now because of the fact that they invaded and took over the wealth of the countries that they have now become. With this view, he saw the wealth of America not as a result of hard work, followed by numerous failures, then more hard work, eventually succeeding, as we see in all successful capitalistic nations. He saw this as an unjust power grab. It absolutely permeated his thinking to the point where he became a political activist **to make sure** that the scales of justice were leveled. It was his goal to **undo all of the injustices** that have brought America to the point where it was when he took over as President of the United States.

This is why President Obama declared words to this effect a few years ago to people who have built businesses, "You didn't build that business! It was the government that allowed you to do what you did." In other words he was saying that **you do not deserve** the fruitage of your labor. This is a socialist idea and the has always been the basis of socialist society. It is also why Socialist countries always end up as failures. There is no motivation to work hard to build something under the realization that you who have worked hard will never be able to enjoy the benefits of your hard work. It will be divided up equally, and much of your hard work will be enjoyed by those who did nothing. This was even tried by the Pilgrims who came here in 1620. They found out very quickly that this does not work.

This is why Rush Limbaugh stated that our values are under assault. According to the Obama philosophy, if you stole what you have, then you deserve to have it taken away from you, or at least it should be completely under the control of the government, to protect it from the injustices of a Capitalistic society. As a result of this, his idea was to shrink the **power** of America on the worldwide stage, and increase the power of the **government** over the people on the American stage. Only this would be able to keep these injustices from running rampant.

I believe it was his desire to **downgrade** America and **upgrade** the more underdeveloped nations of the world in order to sort of balance the scales of justice. One of the ways he has managed to accomplish this is by going on a spending spree. His spending spree increased the national debt **more than all other administrations in American history COMBINED!** When Obama took over as President, the national debt stood at $10,000,000,000,000 (Ten Trillion Dollars). When he left office in January of 2017, it was approximately $20,000,000,000,000 (Twenty Trillion Dollars). If you think about it, this will work by reducing the power of America financially. It is working as America is becoming more and more subservient to its creditors.

Is it any wonder that Donald Trump campaigned on the phrase: "Make America Great Again?" Obama's directive was to make America smaller, and more subservient to other nations. By creating all of that debt in America, Obama also knew that it would make America smaller because the youth of America would be saddled with that debt for a very long time. That debt is now owed to many other nations like China, who is now beginning to challenge America for the top spot economically. Having said all of that, if Obama was nothing else, he was a good salesman. He was instrumental in a sale of a more radical shift to the left of our media, schools, and institutions of learning than any other President in the course of history. Can we undo the assault that Obama portrayed on the American people? That remains to be seen. Obama was very successful in changing the ideology of America especially with the youth during his eight years in office.

Fortunately for us Hillary Clinton lost the election and Donald Trump won. Although we cannot say that Donald Trump is a conservative in every respect of the term, (in fact we know he is liberal in some of his ideology) we know that it is his stated goal to return this country to its financial, and military dominance that has been the case in its past.

## The Future of Conservatism in America

The future of conservatism in America is very suspect. The Obama years changed so much of what we know for the liberal agenda that we do not know if it can be recovered. The Left turn in America has been drastic. Our political system is, right now as I write these words, deeply imbedded with people whose ideology is like this. I am speaking of people who are radicals. People who are corrupt enough to ignore our laws and do as they please. This has been shown by judges who **legislate from the bench**. They are making rulings that **completely ignore** our laws and completely support their radical ideology. This was recently shown by the way a federal judge in

Hawaii decided on his own that the statute giving the President the authority to create the temporary travel ban on certain countries with a history of terrorism was of no effect. Thus he slapped a halt on it, **not** in accordance with law, but on the basis of what the president said in his campaign speeches. This practice is called legislating from the bench. The separation of powers was created to stop this. Judges are **required** to make their decisions on the basis of the statutes and laws of the United States and not on the basis of their ideological beliefs.

It has been shown in the way the professors of our institutions of higher learning have moved even further left than before. As such, they have been successful in training our youth to falsely believe that the liberal agenda is the correct and the more moral agenda.

The liberals have convinced the youth of America that they have the correct way of thinking in a whole host of important issues. They have been led to believe that liberals are for the little guy and help minority groups, immigrants, the less fortunate, and women, but conservatives hate them. Nothing could be further from the truth. The fact is that liberals **always exploit** these groups.

By convincing the youth that they are the ideology of the future, the liberal teachers and professors are poisoning our youth. Turning this around will be difficult because these educators are firmly entrenched in the institutions of higher learning. The liberals also control the mainstream media. With both of these in their arsenal of power, we know that this means that it will be very difficult to keep liberal ideology from continuing to dominate in the future.

With Donald Trump as President, and with the hatred that the media has for him, it seems that the only way the tide can be turned in this arena is for him to be successful in reversing the things that he campaigned on, and for it to be **so successful** that the media can no longer ignore his success. Time will tell. Even though President Trump is not a conservative in all of his ideas, he is much more so than the liberal media and schools.

Most young people are totally ignorant about conservatism. Outside of talk radio and Fox News there are few media outlets that will help them to understand the importance of the values that American conservatives espouse.

There is no doubt that the mainstream media is the biggest enemy of conservatism. I would highly implore you to look at the appendix which shows a sample email letter that you can use to send to your Senator and your representatives to **demand an investigation** into these media atrocities. Please take action on this matter. **It is up to us** to do this or it will never get done. You can also call your representatives and Senators. But flooding their email inboxes seems to me to be more effective.

As we go forward to look at Racism in America today, we will see that it is a force that is truly contrary to our values. Lincoln was keenly aware of this, and it was the reason he forced the issue. But what is the truth about Racism and its background. In the next chapter we will look at this in depth.

# Racism, Slavery, and Fascism

**Where and with whom did these ideals begin?**

**Where do we see these ideals exhibited today?**

As I write this today in March of 2017, I can tell you that if you listen to the liberal media often enough, you cannot help but hear the term Fascist or Fascism. Usually this is used in reference to the Republicans or the Conservatives. Since Donald Trump won the Election, and pretty much declared an all-out war on the Mainstream media, we hear a lot of trash talk about him and he is often referred to as a fascist. This begs the questions: What is Fascism? What are Fascists? How does this tie to the Racism which has recently flared up in America?

This chapter will be historical in nature. It will not be long, but it will show that it is clear from history that the Democrat Party was the party of slavery, racism, and fascism from the time of its formation under Andrew Jackson, throughout the time of the Civil War, and has continued to work for these ideals in a subversive way even to this day despite their denials and the denials of the media. The information I am presenting to you is shocking. Please follow it to its end....it won't take that long and you will be glad you did.

The Miriam Webster dictionary defines Fascism as follows:

1. *1 often capitalized* : a political philosophy, movement, or regime (as that of the Fascisti) that exalts nation and often race above the individual and that stands for a centralized autocratic government headed by a dictatorial leader, severe economic and social regimentation, and forcible suppression of opposition
2. *2* : a tendency toward or actual exercise of strong autocratic or dictatorial control

As we can see, this does, in fact, tie Fascism to Racism. Adolf Hitler was a Fascist, and it was obvious that he was a racist. He exalted people who were blond haired and blue eyed to the top of the spectrum. At the bottom of the spectrum were the Jews, of which he ordered the execution of six million. Mussolini was a Fascist, but he was different than Hitler.

He created a party known as the National Fascist Party in 1919. He moved to Switzerland to promote Socialism and was thrown out, returning to Italy where he was able to bring himself up to the point where he became a dictator of the country. Needless to say, this term being associated with these two horrific leaders has promoted the term "fascism" to the point of being known as something undesirable. The term has been overused in our society lately, meaning a bad thing, and not necessarily as it is defined.

As you can see from the Miriam Webster definition, Fascism is tied to racism. When we think of racism in America we know that it roots itself in the history of slavery. Anyway, these terms are often tied together.

Since the next section will deal with specific Presidents and time frames, I am inserting a table here which shows the Presidents in order, with their dates of service, and party affiliation.

| President | Dates Served | Party Affiliation |
|---|---|---|
| 1. George Washington | 1789-1797 | None |
| 2. John Adams | 1797-1801 | Federalist |
| 3. Thomas Jefferson | 1801-1809 | Democratic-Republican |
| 4. James Madison | 1809-1817 | Democratic-Republican |
| 5. James Monroe | 1817-1825 | Democratic-Republican |
| 6. John Quincy Adams | 1825-1829 | Democratic-Republican |
| 7. Andrew Jackson | 1829-1837 | Democrat |
| 8. Martin Van Buren | 1837-1841 | Democrat |
| 9. William Henry Harrison | 1841-1841 (died in office) | Whig |
| 10. John Tyler | 1841-1845 | Unaffiliated |
| 11. James K. Polk | 1845-1849 | Democrat |
| 12. Zachary Taylor | 1849-1850 (died in office) | Whig |
| 13. Millard Fillmore | 1850-1853 | Whig |
| 14. Franklin Pierce | 1853-1857 | Democrat |
| 15. James Buchanan | 1857-1861 | Democrat |
| 16. Abraham Lincoln | 1861-1865 (assassinated) | Republican |
| 17. Andrew Johnson | 1865-1869 | Democrat |
| 18. Ulysses S. Grant | 1869-1877 | Republican |
| 19. Rutherford B. Hayes | 1877-1881 | Republican |
| 20. James A. Garfield | 1881-1881 (died in office) | Republican |
| 21. Chester A. Arthur | 1881-1885 | Republican |
| 22. Grover Cleveland | 1885-1889 | Democrat |
| 23. Benjamin Harrison | 1889-1893 | Republican |
| 24. Grover Cleveland | 1893-1897 | Democrat |

| 25. William McKinley | 1897-1901 | Republican |
|---|---|---|
| 26. Theodore Roosevelt | 1901-1909 | Republican |
| 27. William Howard Taft | 1909-1913 | Republican |
| 28. Woodrow Wilson | 1913-1921 | Democrat |
| 29. Warren G. Harding | 1921-1923 (died in office) | Republican |
| 30. Calvin Coolidge | 1923-1929 | Republican |
| 31. Herbert Hoover | 1929-1933 | Republican |
| 32. Franklin D. Roosevelt | 1933-1945 | Democrat |
| 33. Harry S. Truman | 1945-1953 | Democrat |
| 34. Dwight D. Eisenhower | 1953-1961 | Republican |
| 35. John F. Kennedy | 1961-1963 (assassinated) | Democrat |
| 36. Lyndon B. Johnson | 1963-1969 | Democrat |
| 37. Richard Nixon | 1969-1973 (Resigned) | Republican |
| 38. Gerald Ford | 1974-1977 | Republican |
| 39. Jimmy Carter | 1977-1981 | Democrat |
| 40. Ronald Reagan | 1981-1989 | Republican |
| 41. George H. W. Bush | 1989-1993 | Republican |
| 42. Bill Clinton | 1993-2001 | Democrat |
| 43. George W. Bush | 2001-2009 | Republican |
| 44. Barack Obama | 2009-2017 | Democrat |
| 45. Donald J. Trump | 2017- | Republican |

## Andrew Jackson and the Democrat Party

In order to understand the beginnings of slavery and racism in this country we must get to the roots. It is necessary to go back to the seventh President of the United States. That would be

Andrew Jackson who was the founder of the Democrat Party, and one of the wealthiest slave owners in the country. In a series of articles written by William P. Meyers, he stated:

> Andrew Jackson would grow up to be a President of the United States of America and the founder of the Democratic Party. Along the way **he would murder many of his fellow men and live a life of depravity unmatched,** so far as we know, by any other American President.[14] (emphasis mine)

This is a very serious allegation. But is it true? On the surface, we might not think this to be true. . Although much has been written about Andrew Jackson, most of it is positive. But there was a shady side of President Jackson that is seldom revealed.

His Presidency came after his military service in which he was a Major-General. He became famous through his aggressive actions against Indians in

---

14

http://www.iiipublishing.com/politics/us/jackson/election_1824.html, much of this information was taken from *The Life of Andrew Jackson* by Marquis James, Bobbs-Merrill company, 1938.

the Indian wars. He was not a man of means, but was a good politician. He entered the U.S. Senate in 1797, but resigned after one year, pleading financial difficulties. But history showed that these financial difficulties **were soon to be reversed** in a big way.

In 1802, Jackson was elected Major-General of the Tennessee militia, and he retained that post through the War of 1812. This would be the beginning of the means by which Major-General Jackson would become wealthy. Through a series of land deals, Andrew Jackson forced several tribes of Indians westward including the tribes of the Creeks, the Cherokees, the Chicksaws, the Choctaws, and the Seminoles. He did this despite the fact that he painstakingly convinced these tribes that their migration would be voluntary, an out and out lie. He therefore made treaties with them that would not be kept, and many fraudulent land deals were made.

In his book, *The Long Bitter Trail: Andrew Jackson and the Indians,* Historian Anthony Wallace explains that President Jackson was in charge of **a ruthlessly destructive policy** with regard to these native Americans that resulted in the **destruction of their culture**, and ended up forcing them off of their land. Jackson, who was heretofore **not** wealthy, through his position and the manipulation of these unscrupulous land deals he gradually became **very** wealthy.[15]

Prior to his first failed run for the Presidency in 1824, with the immense wealth that he had obtained, Jackson purchased a big plantation outside of Nashville, TN. This is where he lived out much of his life as a wealthy slave owner. He ran again and was successfully elected as president in 1828, after which he kicked the Indians out of their ancestral land east of the Mississippi river and located them west of the Mississippi. Jackson's Plantation was big. His mansion was extensive and he was served well by his slaves which numbered over 150. He had a massive stable which included fifty horses, and hundreds of livestock.[16]

## The Civil War, Slavery and the Democrat Party

Although the Civil War has been known to be a war of the Northern States verses the Southern

---

[15] Wallace, Anthony (2011-03-31T23:58:59). The Long, Bitter Trail: Andrew Jackson and the Indians (Hill and Wang Critical Issues) (Kindle Locations 79-80). Farrar, Straus and Giroux. Kindle Edition.

[16] Ibid. Kindle Locations 79-80

states, with the North being opposed to slavery verses the South being for slavery. But a closer examination reveals that this war was more of a Republican verses Democrat war. Here are some facts that I would like to call to your attention:

1.  The Republican Party had its beginnings with its first anti-slavery Presidential candidate John C. Freemont. Although he lost on his strong anti-slavery agenda, the next Republican candidate to run under such an agenda, Abraham Lincoln did win the election, bringing about the changes that led to the Civil War. Before he even took office seven mostly Democratic States seceded from the Union forcing Lincoln's hand. They hated Lincoln so much that Democrat John Wilkes Booth assassinated him after the war ended.

2.  The 13th amendment, abolishing slavery took place in 1864. the vote was passed in the Senate by a vote of 38 to 6. The final vote showed that support for its passage came almost exclusively from the Republicans. The vote included 30 Republicans, 4 from Democrats, 3 from unionists, and 1 from an Unconditional Unionist.[17]

---

[17]

3. Since there was a 2/3 majority required for a new amendment to pass, the house came up 13 votes short of a passage. The House of Representatives did not pass the Bill until 10 months later after Lincoln was re-elected as President with a 55% majority. The House passed the Thirteenth amendment by a vote of 119-56 with the Republicans mostly supporting and the Democrats mostly against it.[18]

4. The 14th amendment which addresses equal protections of rights of all citizens was written to allow such privileges to the former slaves. It passed by a majority of the Republicans and was opposed by a majority of the Democrats. It was passed by a 2/3 majority by mostly Republicans but under a lot of controversy and was ratified by the states. It became a legal amendment on July 9, 1868.

5. The 15th amendment provided voting rights to blacks was passed by a Republican majority with the House voting 144 to 44, and the Senate voting 39 to 13. In both cases, it was the Republican majority which prevailed.

---

https://en.wikipedia.org/wiki/Thirteenth_Amendment_to_the_United_States_Constitution

[18] https://www.ourdocuments.gov/doc.php?flash=true&doc=40

## Ku Klux Klan and the Democrat Party

The Ku Klux Klan was an arm of the Democrat Party and was formed in the mid-1860's when the 13th and 14th amendments were being considered. Its mission was to disrupt all of these proceedings, and oust the Republicans who were in control of most of the State governments. Note the following quote:

> The original targets of the Ku Klux Klan were Republicans, both black and white, according to a new television program and book, which describe how the Democrats started the KKK and for decades harassed the GOP with lynchings and threats.

> An estimated 3,446 blacks and 1,297 whites died at the end of KKK ropes from 1882 to 1964.

> The documentation has been assembled by David Barton of Wallbuilders and published in his book "Setting the Record Straight: American History in Black & White," which reveals that not only did the Democrats work hand-in-glove with the Ku Klux Klan for

generations, they started the KKK and endorsed its mayhem.

"Of all forms of violent intimidation, lynchings were by far the most effective," Barton said in his book. "Republicans often led the efforts to pass federal anti-lynching laws and their platforms consistently called for a ban on lynching.[19]

The KKK movement was suppressed by federal law enforcement in the early 1870's and pretty much was dissolved except for a few die-hards. It re-emerged in the mid 1910's with many of the same white supremacist ideas. Both of these organizations were created by Democrats.

After the Lincoln assassination, Andrew Johnson, his Vice President took over. Since he was a Democrat, he did not have any supporters of the reconstruction in his administration. He showed his racism when he stated:

---

[19]

https://www.liveleak.com/view?i=502_1193356283#SGIVKX8d
dzUJ1gWp.99

"This is **a country for white men**," he had reportedly declared, "and as long as I am president, it shall be a government **for white men**."[20]

He fired the Secretary of War, Edwin M. Stanton. But congress overruled him. Johnson ignored this and formally dismissed him anyway. The House of Representatives made the decision, and formally **impeached him** on February 24 by a vote of 126 to 47. Their charge was that he brought "disgrace, ridicule, hatred, contempt, and reproach to the Congress of the United States.

From the time of Andrew Johnson until the time of Woodrow Wilson the office of the President of the United States was controlled by Republicans with the exception of Grover Cleveland's two administrations.

But Grover Cleveland **continued** the Democrat Legacy of **racism** and called the Reconstruction a failed experiment. Thus, he **refused to support the 15th Amendment** of the United States Constitution, which guaranteed voting rights to black Americans. He also would not appoint them

---

[20]

http://www.pbs.org/wgbh/americanexperience/features/general-article/grant-impeachment/

to any political patronage jobs with the exception of Fredrick Douglass who was a Recorder of Deeds in Washington D.C.[21]

Grover Cleveland was succeeded in the Presidency by Benjamin Harrison who served between Cleveland's two terms. William McKinley, Theodore Roosevelt, and William Howard Taft, were all Republicans.

## Woodrow Wilson's Administration

As we approach the presidency of Woodrow Wilson, we will explore the racist and white supremacist ideas he promoted. When Wilson came into the White House, as was the usual custom, many positions of servitude were changed. In other words, many, if not all, Republicans were fired. But many of these were black people. As there were most likely no black people in the Democrat party, when his house staff fired the black civil servants, they were replaced with white people. This in effect undermined any vestiges of a black middle class in Washington. In his book *Racism in the Nation's Service: Government Workers and the Color Line in Woodrow Wilson's*

---

[21] http://potus-geeks.livejournal.com/162119.html

*America,* Eric Yellin points out that Wilson's desire in his discrimination of civil service positions was to limit them, control them and exploit them. Under this system, they would get paid less and have less upward mobility.

It is noteworthy that under the previous Republican administrations of McKinley through Taft there were many blacks in civil service positions. But under the new Democrat administration headed up by Wilson, there would be none of that. It was Wilson's officials who ran the administration and many of these men were noted white supremacists from his own party who created and executed these plans. Notice Yellin's research concerning this:

> Wilson's government was no more racialized (that is, involved in maintaining racial categories and distinctions) than preceding administrations, but it was more dedicated to white supremacy. By denying appointments, promotions, and even dignity to African American workers, Wilsonians limited the ability of African Americans to obtain stable employment and build the kind of wealth, not just income, that is required to rise in

American society. The attrition of African American clerks in federal offices was not simply a routine political purging of loyal Republicans at the hands of newly empowered Democrats. It was a deliberate subversion of a small but growing class of African American middle-class professionals. Under a segregationist regime, being black meant being economically vulnerable, just as it meant suffering social and political inequality.[22]

## Franklin D. Roosevelt to Lyndon B. Johnson

After Woodrow Wilson left the office of the Presidency, and prior to the Presidency of Franklin D. Roosevelt, three more Republicans were in office including Warren G. Harding, Calvin Coolidge, and Herbert Hoover. Franklin D. Roosevelt came into office in the middle of the Great Depression. He took many drastic measures to reverse this depression, but that is not the focus of this chapter.

---

[22] Yellin, Eric S. (2013-04-21T23:58:59). Racism in the Nation's Service: Government Workers and the Color Line in Woodrow Wilson's America (Kindle Locations 177-185). The University of North Carolina Press. Kindle Edition.

From looking into his thinking in the 1930's, it appears that he was fascinated with Fascism. Note this as written by the Cato Institute.

In the North American Review in 1934, the progressive writer Roger Shaw described the New Deal as "Fascist means to gain liberal ends." He wasn't hallucinating. FDR's adviser Rexford Tugwell wrote in his diary that Mussolini had done "many of the things which seem to me necessary." Lorena Hickok, a close confidante of Eleanor Roosevelt who lived in the White House for a spell, wrote approvingly of a local official who had said, "If [President] Roosevelt were actually a dictator, we might get somewhere." She added that if she were younger, she'd like to lead "the Fascist Movement in the United States." At the National Recovery Administration (NRA), the cartel-creating agency at the heart of the early New Deal, one report declared forthrightly, "The Fascist Principles are very similar to those we have been evolving here in America."

Roosevelt himself called Mussolini "admirable" and professed that he was "deeply impressed by what he has accomplished." The admiration was mutual. In a laudatory review of Roosevelt's 1933 book Looking Forward, Mussolini wrote, "Reminiscent of Fascism is the principle that the state no longer leaves the economy to its own devices.... Without question, the mood accompanying this sea change resembles that of Fascism." The chief Nazi newspaper, *Volkischer Beobachter*, repeatedly praised "Roosevelt's adoption of National Socialist strains of thought in his economic and social policies" and "the development toward an authoritarian state" based on the "demand that collective good be put before individual self-interest."[23]

President Roosevelt also seemed to have an affinity for Adolf Hitler. Notice what was recorded recently from an article in the Daily Caller

In fact, at his first inauguration address, Roosevelt practically adapted the verbiage of Europe's ominous strong-men for the more ironic and irreverent American lexicon — but the anti-democratic substance is easy to identify all the same:

---

[23] https://www.cato.org/publications/commentary/hitler-mussolini-roosevelt

*If we are to go forward, we must move as a trained and loyal army willing to sacrifice for the good of a common discipline. We are, I know, ready and willing to submit our lives and property to such discipline, because it makes possible a leadership which aims at a larger good. I assume unhesitatingly the leadership of this great army ... I shall ask the Congress for the one remaining instrument to meet the crisis — broad executive power to wage a war against the emergency, as great as the power that would be given to me if we were in fact invaded by a foreign foe.*

Words like this would work just as well in Nuremberg square.

Liberals are either delusional or willfully disingenuous when they conduct character assassinations of Republican standard-bearers based on flimsy comparisons to "Hitler."

But it is infinitely better to be compared to a leftist caricature of Hitler than to vocally support the **actual** Hitler, as so many

Democrats did when he was a living, breathing threat to humanity.[24]

FDR in passing the New Deal made a deal with the devil in his compromises. In order to get support for the bill he agreed to block all lynching laws proposed by the Republicans, as a caveat to get the support of his fellow racist Democrats. Additionally, the New Deal was to exclude the working programs most used by black people. By this, I mean that FDR did not put anything in the New Deal for Agricultural Labor and Domestic Service

After World War II and Harry Truman's administration, Dwight D. Eisenhower was elected the President of The United States, followed by John F. Kennedy. Kennedy also seemed to have a fascination with Hitler which he revealed in his diary. Several News outlets are reporting about this even as I write these words. Note this report by CBS News:

> When JFK was writing about Hitler, the dictator's suicide had happened just four months earlier, reports CBS News correspondent Tony Dokoupil. It shows a

---

[24] http://dailycaller.com/2016/12/13/fdr-praised-mussolini-and-loved-fascism/

side of Kennedy we've never seen before.

Some two decades before addressing crowds in West Berlin as president, Kennedy wrote 61 diary pages – 12 in long-hand, 49 typed – in the summer of 1945. Germany had just surrendered, and Kennedy was touring Europe as a newspaper correspondent, traveling shoulder to shoulder with leaders from around the world.

The young JFK's final destination was Germany, just months after the Allied victory. Already a scholar on global politics, Kennedy seems fascinated with Hitler and his place in history, writing: "He had in him the stuff of which legends are made" and "within a few years Hitler will emerge from the hatred that surrounds him now as one of the most significant figures who ever lived."

"There's no glorification, and I wouldn't take this out of context," said Bobby Livingston, executive vice president of RR Auction, the auction house offering the diary. "I think Kennedy was a historian, and he's writing his understanding of Hitler's place in history."

Kennedy wrote Hitler "had boundless ambition for his country which rendered him a menace to the peace of the world, but he had a mystery about him in the way he lived and in the manner of his death that will live and grow after him."[25]

I think it is strange that Kennedy would be fascinated with someone who ordered the execution of six million Jews. Is there an underlying reason for this? I know that JFK was a popular President, but there is no doubt that Hitler was perhaps the most extreme racist ever known to man. Don't you think he would want to distance himself as much as possible from him? It could be that even though he would publicly deny anything like this, since he wrote this in his personal diary, this seemed to indicate his real thinking concerning this horrific leader.

## LBJ and the Big Party Switch

There are many Democrats who agree with all of this history and will say that it is not relevant today because of an idea called "The Big Party Switch." Under this theory, all of a sudden, the Democrats became enlightened about racial equality in the nineteen sixties under the Lyndon B. Johnson administration, and the Democrats who were still racists suddenly became

---

[25] http://www.cbsnews.com/news/jfk-john-f-kennedy-diary-auction-thoughts-on-adolf-hitler/

Republicans. Now I have to be persuaded that just to say such a thing seems ridiculous. People's ideas do not change that way. Why would the American people "suddenly" change their political party?

The fact is that there was a party change somewhere during a longer period in the 1950's or the 1960's but the reasons remain controversial. Dinesh Dsouza who created the movie "Hillary's America" noted that the switch for the blacks to the Democrat party are the result of the policies of the New Deal, and the only racist that did switch parties from Democrat to Republican during this time period was Senator Strom Thurmond.

Mark Levin confirmed much of this, and noted that the President Lyndon B. Johnson **did** propose the 1964 Civil Rights Act, but was **unable to get his party to back him** on it. Maybe it's because LBJ himself voted against Anti-lynching laws as a Senator. So what was the motive in putting this law, The Civil Rights Act of 1964, before Congress? Was it because President Johnson saw the light, and truly had a change of heart?

Mark Levin continued to note in his radio address:

> Considering the history of the parties, it should not be a surprise that the Republican House voted for The Civil Rights Act of 1964 by a margin of 87% Republican to 61%

Democrats. In the Senate, 82% of the Republicans voted for it, 69% of the Democrats voted against it. Among those who voted against it were Al Gore Sr., Robert Bird, and William Fulbright. Robert Bird eventually became the majority leader of the Democrat Party. Even though 1964 Republican candidate Barry Goldwater was against this Bill, but he was certainly not a racist and supported two previous attempts at passage which were **overwhelmingly opposed by Democrats**.

He was the founding member of the Arizona chapter of the NAACP. Levin notes that he hired many blacks in his family business and moved to desegregate the Arizona National Guard. He opposed Johnson's Bill because he believed some elements of it were unconstitutional. Levin continues in saying that the change of parties began in the 1950's in response to economic developments in the Cold War. Black voters in the North began to abandon the party in response to the New Deal of FDR. But many Southern White Democrats changed party affiliation with General Eisenhower's election.[26]

---

[26] https://www.youtube.com/watch?v=2RBFOTdY1yY

But from my investigation of the change in party of blacks from Republican to Democrat, it all has to do with the provisions of the Great Society Program which LBJ promoted and got passed into law. Here is what the Black Republican blog states:

> Contrary to popular belief, President Lyndon Johnson did not predict a racist exodus to the Republican Party from the Democratic Party because of Johnson's support of the Civil Rights Act of 1964. Omitted from the Democrats' rewritten history is what Johnson actually meant by his prediction.

> Johnson feared that the racist Democrats would again form a third party, such as the short-lived States Rights Democratic Party. In fact, Alabama's Democrat Governor George C. Wallace in 1968 started the American Independent Party that attracted other racist candidates, including the Democrat Governor of Georgia, Lester Maddox.

> Behind closed doors, Johnson said: "These Negroes, they're getting uppity these days. That's a problem for us, since they got something now they never had before. The political pull to back up their upityness. Now, we've got to do something about this.

We've got to give them a little something. Just enough to quiet them down, but not enough to make a difference. If we don't move at all, their allies will line up against us. And there'll be no way to stop them. It'll be Reconstruction all over again."

Little known by many today is the fact that it was Republican Senator Everett Dirksen from Illinois, not Johnson, who pushed through the 1964 Civil Rights Act. In fact, Dirksen was instrumental to the passage of civil rights legislation in 1957, 1960, 1964, 1965 and 1968. Dirksen wrote the language for the 1965 Voting Rights Act. Dirksen also crafted the language for the Civil Rights Act of 1968 which prohibited discrimination in housing.[27]

These social programs that were passed in the 1960's included many programs for the failed "War on Poverty" programs, and the many welfare related programs that were passed. These included new disability provisions for Social Security, and the passage of the Food Stamp Act of 1964 and other freebies which were provided later such as

---

[27] http://blackrepublican.blogspot.com/2012/06/republicans-and-democrats-did-not.html

D. Robert Pike Ph.D

free contraceptives, and meal programs for low-income seniors. Republicans opposed these programs because they constitute a new kind of slavery which ties many black and low income Americans to becoming bound to the state in their dependence.

Thus, because of this opposition, Republicans have been called fascists and racists. But here are the facts we learn from history. Fascists are totally opposed to Free Market Capitalism, and believe in political violence to achieve their goals. Remember the Occupy Wall Street movement? It was grounded in violent anarchism to make their statement. Mussolini believed in a State regulated government which would bring "hope and change" (does that sound familiar?) to the people through similar politically violent means.

The name for the Nazi party was actually the National Socialist Workers Party, and we all know the outcome of this regime; Yes, just another failed socialist regime, just like the USSR failure years later. The Nazi Party was racist to the core, and promulgated a Totalitarian Socialist Agenda. Please consider carefully the following question: Which political party today is in favor of big government, big regulation, and a highly socialistic culture?

So after fifty years of these programs that were begun by the Democrats, including the failed "War on Poverty" program, are these less fortunate ones better or worse off? History has shown that now **they are worse off**, having now created a culture wherein generations keep on living off of these government programs instead of pulling themselves out of this brand of slavery and becoming productive members of Society.

Donald Trump, who just recently became President, appealed in his campaign to these black inner city voters to the fact that none of these programs have worked and that they had nothing to lose by voting for him.

As we conclude this chapter we note that these liberal socialistic policies are what has marked the Democratic Party for the past fifty years. As time has passed, these policies have become more and more liberal. These ideals of the Democrat party will be more fully explored in the next chapter.

# Liberal America

The book of Luke records that when Jesus returned to his hometown of Nazareth, he went to the synagogue and said the following:

> **Luke 4:18** "The Spirit of the Lord is upon me, because he has anointed me to proclaim good news to the poor. He has sent me to proclaim liberty to the captives and recovering of sight to the blind, to set at liberty those who are oppressed," (ESV)

This might be similar to a cry of a liberal who claims to be religious (although it is doubtful that he will profess Christ). He might say: "Aren't we doing just as Jesus did? We are trying to help those less fortunate than ourselves." Sounds good, doesn't it? It would be good if it were true. **It is not**.

We are living in a very liberal society. Now what I am speaking of here is not liberalism as we learned from the philosophers of Europe.

## The beginning of liberal thought

When we think about the early beginnings of Liberal thought you must include $17^{th}$ century English philosopher John Locke as one of the most influential in this arena and is widely regarded as the Father of liberalism. His basic premise was that at the beginning of life we have a blank slate, which means we have no innate ideas. So the implication of this is that man is not predisposed to have an innate belief in God. This is contrary to prominent philosophers Plato and Descartes who expounded the belief that man is born with innate ideas, knowledge and beliefs.

The origin of philosophy is attributed to Plato who existed hundreds of years before the time of Christ. Rene Descartes was a $17^{th}$ century philosopher who preceded John Locke. Plato and Rene Descartes both emphasized that the key to unlocking these innate points of knowledge is by having the experiences of life in the early years of human life. Both of these philosophers proclaimed that these innate ideas in the mind of the human have been placed there by God, and that man is predisposed to be of faith in a Creator as opposed to no predisposition at all. In the case of Plato, many of the ideas he promoted in his ideal city were socialistic in nature, and provided a foundation for many of these philosophies today, such as Marxism, and similar ideologies found in the Islamic faith and others.

Following in the footsteps of John Locke was philosopher David Hume. David Hume was known as one of the biggest skeptics in the realm of philosophy. Thus he was skeptical of God and rejected the truth of any revealed religion. He further claimed that religion had harmful consequences to society. From his perspective there were no rational arguments that could lead us to a Creator.

Thus with these beginnings, the educational institutions of higher learning became more and more Godless. Skepticism has since become the order of the day, and the mindset of the Liberals is that the more rational thinkers are considered to be either atheists or agnostics. But this gives rise to the question, if there is no Creator, what is the basis of our morality? Yes, that's right....there is **NO** basis for morality. That explains why we see such vitriol spewing from the mouths of Liberals. It explains why the rich Liberal elitists are willing to hire anarchists to destroy property at protests. It explains why the Liberal agenda of the US

Congress and Senate right now is to delay, distort, and disrupt our newly elected President to keep him from carrying out his agenda.

In another Barna research poll we see the effect of the educational institutions on people.[28]

## Mostly Conservative on Social and Political Issues

- Evangelicals: 64%
- Non-Evangelical, Born Again: 34%
- Notional Christians: 25%
- Non-Christian Faith: 16%
- Atheist/Agnostic: 4%

So from this we see that there are very few Atheists and Agnostics that subscribe to any conservative thought

It is important that the term liberalism is not confused with libertarianism. Actually the two are practically opposing terms. What I am about to describe is not about uninformed people....those ones that Rush Limbaugh describes as low information voters. These ones are those who have

---

[28] https://www.thoughtco.com/liberal-atheists-vs-conservative-christians-247834

been misled by the dishonest liberal media, and have not done their homework in finding out the truth. The truth is that the Liberal mainstream media puts a liberal spin on most of the "news" that they report. This has been very successful in misleading vast numbers of people in this nation.

In this country, liberalism is based on freedom in social issues, with flair to the dishonest premise of over coddling of the less fortunate. This is taken to extreme to the point where the liberals know that those who are lazy take advantage of the system and always have their hand out and will remain subservient. The liberals got to this position by its early beginnings, most likely with the **New Deal** which was a program of Franklin D. Roosevelt. This resulted in an explosion of government sponsored programs which now include Social Security, Medicare, Federal Crop insurance, the Federal Housing administration. Various welfare programs in this country now include such things as Aid to Dependent Children, Medicaid, Supplemental Security Income, and unemployment insurance.

While many of these programs **ARE** beneficial, many are abused. Social Security and Medicare have been forced upon us for decades, and subsequently have become the **main staples** of seniors **of which I am included**. For people in the United States, there is no choice in the participation in these programs. Everyone **must** participate. The reason that it is a problem today is that it was started as the world's biggest Ponzi scheme. Those who benefitted at first did not put anything into the program. As it has grown throughout the years it appears that the ones which will be hurt the worst are those future beneficiaries who will not be able to be supported without drastic cutbacks in benefits. These are programs that appear to be doomed to drastic downsizing and reduced benefits to those who will pay the most and for the longest time.

Opposing this is the concept of libertarianism, which is basically a political philosophy that upholds the right to the liberty of the individual as a core principle. Now although these may sound somewhat similar to liberal principles, the difference is that Libertarians uphold to the highest degree the principle of self-ownership. In this political philosophy, the core principles to be upheld are autonomy, and political freedom. This a basic tenant of conservatism.

This is the opposite of liberalism. Liberals put on the façade of believing that everyone should be supported by a huge government which makes everyone equal regardless of socio-economic background or education. This is in effect a falsehood. Most of the liberal elitists want to keep their elite privileges, and keep the less fortunate suppressed.

Here are some examples:

Big Government liberals push for more welfare and longer unemployment benefits instead of trying to get true and lasting job creation. At the same time they act like they have big hearts, hearts that encompass the care of all less fortunate individuals. But these "handout policies" do much more damage than good. It has resulted in a segment of our society that lives in the welfare state, never even trying to get free from its bondage. Adults in this quagmire end up training their children how to get as many "freebies" as possible while doing the least amount of work.

I remember one occasion when I was renting out a condo to one of those whom I considered as a less fortunate individual. I did everything I could to help him, but instead of being thankful, he treated me as if he was entitled to what he was getting. He was always late paying his utility bills. So one day I wanted to help him out and pay his utility bill for him. He got very angry with me and told me that now he would never be able to qualify for a free service that would have paid this particular bill. In fact, I had to hound him every month for his rent, and finally had to evict him. I never did recover the three months of rent that he owed me. Additionally, he was so lazy that he would not even come and move out his furniture. I finally called the Salvation Army to come and take everything they would. I got rid of the rest.

Our school systems have banned prayer in the schools. They teach the theory of evolution as if it were a fact, but deny the Biblical account of creation. In fact, since I am a member of Gideons International, I know that it used to be that the Gideons were allowed in fifth grade classes all over America to give those children a copy of the New Testament, but now in almost every community in America with a few exceptions, the Gideons must stand on public sidewalks to hand out a copy of God's precious word to them.

Sex crimes in the schools with teachers taking sexual advantage of their students has grown to the point where it is an explosion. How has so much changed? This was unheard of 20 or more years ago! Could it be because of all of the mindless things that are going on in these schools? I am speaking of such things as passing out condoms in class, having explicit classes on such things as sexual performance, even conferences on these things. Is this something that sounds like it would be responsible to teach to adolescents whose minds are still developing? No wonder teen sex is at an all time high.

Back in 2014, there was a conference in Oregon on Adolescent Sexuality. Here are a couple of the workshops that were present in this conference.[29]

*A6 – Breaking Down the Barrier*

*Fyona Rose, Elliot Glaser-Flynn*

This presentation offers insight and tools to help open the difficult conversation of sexuality between adults and youth. During our hour and fifteen minutes we'll be using interactive activities, group discussions, and Q and A's to help audience members break down the walls surrounding youth and sexuality today. After leaving our workshop you'll be armed with the means to start a healthy dialogue about sexuality in your own households and community.

- *Intended Audience: Both Youth & Adults*
- *Main Focus: Gender Identity, Promoting Healthy Relationships, Sexual Health*
- *Level of Information: Intermediate*
- *Presentation Techniques: Lecture, Interactive*

---

[29] http://oregon-asc.org/2015-conference/2014-conference/

B2 – My Mom Wishes I was a Lesbian: "Coming Out" Experiences of (Bi) Sexual Young Adults

1.      *Del Quest, MSW, LCSW*

This workshop will explore some of the unique "coming out" experiences of young adults who are not exclusively gay/lesbian or heterosexual. Participants will learn how a small group of young adults viewed the particular advantages and challenges they experienced as they navigated their social relationships while in high school. We will explore how best to support other young adults who occupy this "middle ground" as they learn to share a coming out story with others.

- *Intended Audience: Youth & Adults*
- *Main Focus: LGBTQ*
- *Level of Information: Intermediate*
- *Presentation Techniques: Interactive*

Does this sound like something you would encourage your adolescent youth to attend? It shows why we have all of these sexual problems in the schools of today.

Now the Biblical principles upon which our American society was formed have been abandoned. This is the result of a multitude of agnostic and atheistic liberal forces and their organizations which have completely squelched these solid principles for upbringing.

In my early years through early adulthood, homosexuality was considered to be contemptable, and despicable, and because of this attitude, it was almost unheard of in mainstream society. Conversely now, those who have come forth professing homosexuality are praised for having courage enough to make themselves known. What has been the effect of such action? It has actually **encouraged** children to become homosexuals! What does God's word say about this?

> Romans 1:27 "and the men likewise gave up natural relations with women and were consumed with passion for one another, men committing shameless acts with men and receiving in themselves the due penalty for their error."

But when Bible verses such as this are brought up, they are mocked, and laughed at. Anyone who brings this up must be a nutty religious fanatic. I find it almost unbelievable but sadly true that society could change in such a short period of time.

Doing still further damage to the message of Christ, it has now become fashionable by the liberal elitists to push any religion except Christianity. The religion which is now being pushed more than any other is Islam which is anything but a liberal religion. What a horrible contradiction on the part of the left. They have pushed aside the truth of the love of Christ, and have given a free pass to a religion that in its most radical form, preaches hate, and suppresses women. It legitimizes such things as beheading, and rape, and don't even think about being a homosexual. Women are treated so poorly in the Muslim countries that they are not even allowed to walk with their husbands, but must walk behind them. In some parts of Muslim society they are not even allowed to show their face, get an education, or drive a car.

On another front we must speak about the insanity of the environmental liberals. By far the greatest country for environmental protection is these United States. By comparison, nations such as China and Russia have been shown to have absolutely pathetic standards of environmental protection. Nonetheless, liberal elitists such as Al Gore preach about how we are destroying the environment just before they get into their Lear jets and put out more carbon emissions in one trip than most people do in a year.

So what do these liberals want to do to give us the power we need to live normal lives? Sorry Al Gore, but you can never fly your airplane with solar power or wind power. What about all of the technology that has been developed to give us more gas and oil? Why is it that Liberals such as Gore continue to push cumbersome new regulations for America while the big cities in China are polluting at a rate twenty times that of US cities? Note the attached comparison between the worst cities in China compared to the worst cities in the USA:

"Small airborne pollutant particles called PM2.5 can harm the lungs when ingested with the potential to cause asthma, cardiovascular disease and cancer. The World Health Organization said that anything over 10 micrograms per cubic meter of PM2.5 should be considered hazardous. China's Ministry of Environmental Protection released a ranking of cities with the worst air pollution, showing the sheer scale of the problem."[30]

---

[30] https://www.forbes.com/sites/niallmccarthy/2015/01/23/air-pollution-chinese-and-american-cities-in-comparison-infographic/#162aa7fc2362

**Air Pollution Levels In Perspective: China And The US**
Daily average particulate pollution (PM2.5) in the 10 worst Chinese and US cities*

| China | | US | |
|---|---|---|---|
| Xingtai | 155.2 | 18.2 | Bakersfield, CA |
| Shijiazhuang | 148.5 | 18.2 | Merced, CA |
| Baoding | 127.9 | 17.0 | Fresno, CA |
| Handan | 127.8 | 16.2 | Hanford, CA |
| Hengshui | 120.6 | 15.3 | Los Angeles, CA |
| Tangshan | 114.2 | 15.2 | Modesto, CA |
| Jinan | 114.0 | 15.0 | Visalia, CA |
| Langfang | 113.8 | 18.2 | Pittsburgh, PA |
| Xi'an | 104.2 | 14.0 | El Centro, CA |
| Zhengzhou | 102.4 | 13.8 | Cincinnati, OH |
| WHO guideline | | 10.0 | |

* Anything over 10 micrograms per cubic meter of PM2.5 considered hazardous to health by WHO

Sources: Washington Post, Chinese Ministry of Environmental Protection, American Lung Association, WHO

**Forbes** statista

There is no doubt that the world got carried away around the end of the 20th century by the panic over global warming, and there is no question that they did everything in their power to provoke the scare by the falsifying of official temperature data. But now another explicit example has been uncovered by Steven Goddard's US blog Real Science, who showed the shamelessness of the left in data manipulation to get the results they want. It involves the graph of US surface temperature records published by the National Oceanic and Atmospheric Administration (NOAA). Note what was done:

> Goddard shows how, in recent years, NOAA's US Historical Climatology Network (USHCN) has been "adjusting" its record by replacing real temperatures with data "fabricated" by

computer models. The effect of this has been to downgrade earlier temperatures and to exaggerate those from recent decades, to give the impression that the Earth has been warming up much more than is justified by the actual data. In several posts headed "Data tampering at USHCN/GISS", Goddard compares the currently published temperature graphs with those based only on temperatures measured at the time. These show that the US has actually been cooling since the Thirties, the hottest decade on record; whereas the latest graph, nearly half of it based on "fabricated" data, shows it to have been warming at a rate equivalent to more than 3 degrees centigrade per century.[31]

Today there are people going to jail for farming their own land which are alleged to be a habitat for some kinds of endangered subspecies of animal. Some are reported to be rotting in prison over the filling in of swamplands on property which they have bought and paid for. Entire communities in the Northwest, including big portions of the timber industry have been deserted and look like ghost towns- because of the wacko environmentalist idea that a White Spotted Owl

---

[31] http://conservativebyte.com/2014/06/lies-environmental-wackos/

can only survive in old growth forest areas. Here are a couple of examples to illustrate the point:

## 75-Year-Old Woman's Plan for Quiet Retirement Dashed by Endangered Species Act

For nearly ten years, Lani Odenthal and her husband Bob worked hard to develop their 80-acre golf course in Okanogan County, Washington into a beautiful, prosperous resort. After Bob passed away in 1998, 75-year-old Lani had no desire to run the Sunny Meadows resort anymore and decided to sell it and live the rest of her life in quiet retirement.

In the spring of 1999, that plan was shattered when the National Marine Fisheries Service (NMFS) ordered the local irrigation company, Skyline Ditch, which served Sunny Meadows and its neighbors, to stop releasing water. Lani's once-lushly-green oasis is now virtually useless as it is now marred by dying brown grass, receding ponds and weedy flower beds.

Citing new Endangered Species Act regulations adopted in early 1999, NMFS alleges that the irrigation provided by Pacific

Northwest water companies, such as Skyline Ditch, harm salmon because it diverts water from streams and rivers vital to salmon survival. NMFS adopted these strict regulations despite serious scientific concerns over whether such regulation of the salmon's freshwater habitat will significantly improve their survivability rates. What is certain, however, is that the denial of vitally-needed water to farmers and other small businesses, such as Lani's golf resort, is having catastrophic consequences.

Soon after Lani decided to sell Sunny Meadows in November 1998, a woman living in the area who frequented Sunny Meadows offered her $1.3 million for the resort - certainly enough for a comfortable retirement. But after the irrigation company cut off the water supply on NMFS's orders, the prospective buyer informed Lani that she couldn't invest when water rights were in doubt.

Stuck with a property she couldn't sell, Lani had to shut down Sunny Meadows as she can no longer offer the golfing, fishing and hiking that once made the resort so popular. To make ends meet, she sold her motor home and other personal belongings. Still, Lani doesn't know if she can pay the rent for her apartment.

Lani says that although her late husband was the kind of man who could find the bright spot in any situation, "I'm just glad he isn't alive to see it today."[32]

Here in my home state of Florida, there are people who have purchased land that is now unusable due to regulations on a certain type of bird. Note the following:

## Florida Man Stuck With Useless Property Because of Federally-Protected Bird

South Florida contractor William Jesberger thought he was taking advantage of a great business opportunity when he purchased two residential lots for $20,000 in order to custom build houses. But in 1992, the U.S. Fish and Wildlife Service (FWS) refused his application for a building permit because his

---

[32]

http://www.propertyrightsresearch.org/endangered_species_hit_list.htm. Here are listed several examples of overreach on this issue.

land was considered vital habitat for the Florida scrub-jay bird which is legally protected as a threatened species by the FWS and the Florida Game and Freshwater Fish Commission. "You can't build on scrub-jay property and the county is assessing property value lower every year because of that," says Jesberger.

Jesberger's ultimate dream has turned into a nightmare. He cannot sell his property because it is deemed a "white elephant." As one realtor aptly stated, "I do not know of any builder that would even want a lot like this as a gift." The lots are completely worthless and Jesberger has been warned to not touch anything on his property or he will be arrested and fined.

Overall, there are 480 lots involved. Jesberger wants to file a class action lawsuit to seek just compensation because "it would be too costly as an individual to go in and sue." Unfortunately, no one else wants to join him; he is the only one that dutifully attends all the meetings on the scrub-jay. Jesberger's case to this day remains at a standstill - he cannot build on his property or sell it as long as the FWS deems it scrub-jay habitat.[33]

Here are two of many examples I could have given of complete and total injustice! See the reference mentioned for more examples of this. When are these people going to realize that the earth was made for man, not man for the earth. This is just another example of the pantheistic beliefs of the left that the creation and the creator are the same. This type of thinking tramples the rights of individuals in order to satisfy the insatiable appetites of uncaring environmentalists.

## First Amendment Rights

## Freedom of Speech

The First Amendment to the Constitution guarantees freedom of speech. But now we want to look at what the liberal mindset is regarding the First Amendment.

Liberals claim to be in favor of the First Amendment. But is this really true? How do they react when the rubber meets the road on this

---

[33] http://www.propertyrightsresearch.org/endangered_species_hit_list.htm

issue? They also claim that they are motivated by love. Michelle Obama said during the presidential election campaign of 2016, "When they take the low road, we take the high road." To reiterate this rhetoric, one of the slogans we saw the liberals carrying on signs in the presidential election won by Donald Trump in 2016 was: **Love trumps Hate!** Let's look into this claim and see its effect on their view of the First Amendment.

Hillary Clinton said that if Donald Trump did not accept the results of the upcoming election that it was "Un-American." And what was the result of the "love trumps hate" campaign? Soon after the elections, anarchists who were bought and paid for by liberal elitists went into Portland Oregon bullying Trump supporters and **destroying property**. Cars and businesses were destroyed. People were **injured**, and businesses were **devastated**. Is this what they meant by **"Love trumps Hate?" Sounds like "Hate trumps Love" to me.** So do they really want freedom of speech protected? Does their view of Freedom of Speech include their right to destroy the property of innocent civilians just because they do not like the outcome of the election?

While these people bring carnage to their destructive campaigns, they always seem to want to tout the virtues of Martin Luther King. But here are some facts which they conveniently ignore.

1. Martin Luther King was a Republican. In those days the KKK were still openly Democrat. It was not until well after LBJ's "big switch" that the KKK abandoned the Democrat party. And that was due to a false narrative purveyed by LBJ indicating that he truly cared for the less fortunate. But history has shown that nothing has changed with respect to the inner urban black community for the past 50 years. They are still in the same situation as they were then, and this is intentional by the Democrat elitists.

2. Martin Luther King advocated peaceful revolution. He would have been outraged at the violence today. All of his protests were peaceful, and he was hated by the Democrat establishment.

3. The family of MLK believed that his murder was the result of a government conspiracy, and they won their case. Note what is reported:

   a. The King family and others believe that the assassination was carried out by a conspiracy involving the U.S.

government, as alleged by Lloyd Jowers in 1993, and that Ray was a scapegoat. In 1999 the King family filed a wrongful death lawsuit against Jowers for the sum of $10,000,000. During closing arguments, the King's attorney asked the jury to award damages of $100.00, to make the point that "it was not about the money." During the trial both the family and Jowers presented evidence alleging a government conspiracy. The government agencies accused could not defend themselves or respond because they were not named as defendants. Based on the evidence, the jury concluded that Jowers and "others were part of a conspiracy to kill King." and awarded $100.00[34]

To those holding those signs, lets further test this "love trumps hate" implication. What about children? Do these liberals love children? What about children about to be born? Here again we

---

34

https://en.wikipedia.org/wiki/Assassination_of_Martin_Luther_King_Jr.

see the falsehood of love being portrayed. Almost without exception, liberals will say that "women have the right to choose." But what about the babies? Do they have the right to choose? **NO!** Why, because they are not considered as anything until **AFTER** they are born.

But behind all of this, there is a belief system. The true Liberals do not believe the American slogan: **"In God we Trust**." In fact many **do not** believe in God! If there is any presiding belief in the mind of any of these people, it is perhaps a belief in Pantheism, which basically is belief that **everything is God**. It is a belief in the deity of the creation instead of the creator. This explains why liberals will go to any extreme to preserve the life of some unknown but recently discovered bird here in Southwest Florida but are in favor of partial birth abortion where a human life is brutally murdered.

Although they put on the guise of freedom of religion, they really don't care about that but demand obeisance to their ideology no matter what religion is "practiced" by its adherents. The real tragedy of this is that now we see this radical ideology running rampant in our school systems. Most universities are completely controlled by liberal ideologies and have few professors who are willing to buck the trend. And as mentioned earlier, prayer in schools is non-existent. Even at sporting events, graduations, and school functions, those who pray publicly are excoriated and usually punished. Even moments of silence for certain reasons are now being oppressed because they know that prayer might occur during these times.

Here is an example of how liberals respect freedom of speech.

> **MARCH 6, 2017** —Violence that erupted at a pro-Trump rally in the famously liberal city of Berkeley, Calif., was the exception, not the norm for the so-called Spirit of America demonstrations in 28 of the nation's 50 states on Saturday.
>
> In downtown Berkeley, Trump supporters clashed with counter-protesters in several fights, a video filmed by Reuters shows. Ten in all were arrested and seven injured in scuffles in the Martin Luther King Jr. Civic Center Park, less than a mile from the University of California, Berkeley campus.
>
> Scattered arrests were made at other rallies on Saturday including in Minnesota and Tennessee. But the general flavor of the day was one of support for President Trump and,

to some, reconciliation, reported The Christian Science Monitor.

The violence came less than a month after masked protesters at the nearby University of California, Berkeley, campus forced the university to cancel a planned speech by white nationalist provocateur Milo Yiannopoulos. Those demonstrators **destroyed property** and **ignited explosives**, prompting a campus lockdown.[35]

I have yet to see **ANY** conservative anarchists. These anarchists from the left almost always keep their faces covered. Now I just want to ask: Why do you think they would do that? This is the action of **cowards** just like the radical Muslim Jihadists they are emulating. Such a thing is not a part of the conservative mindset.

But just how do liberals view freedom of speech? **They want to restrict it.** Back in 2014, they introduced a bill that would do just that. Note the following:

---

[35] http://www.csmonitor.com/USA/2017/0306/Violence-at-Berkeley-rally-but-most-pro-Trump-protests-are-peaceful

An effort is underway in the Senate to amend the Constitution to restrict free speech by allowing Congress to limit fundraising and spending on political speech. A constitutional amendment proposed by Senator Tom Udall (D–NM) would grant Congress the power to regulate the raising and spending of money in elections. Supporters of this amendment claim that restricting the amount of money that may be spent on political speech and activity is *not* the same as limiting speech, even though "virtually every means of communicating ideas in today's mass society requires the expenditure of money."[36]

So what did they try to do here? Their idea was to shut down opposition by reducing the amount of spending that could be done on TV and Radio ads, or mailings. But this was not the first time that such tactics were approached by the Left. Back in 2008, when Hillary Clinton was running for President, a group called Citizens United produced a movie named "Hillary: The Movie" that they wanted to show just prior to the democrat primaries. But the Leftists did everything in their power to stop them from showing it, including obtaining lower court rulings which agreed with them. However when this got to the Supreme

---

[36] http://www.heritage.org/report/amending-the-first-amendment-how-the-campaign-finance-amendment-will-silence-free-speech

Court, the ruling was that this was a restriction of freedom of speech as protected by the First Amendment.

This was the correct ruling. **The First Amendment of the Constitution** is very clear on this. Here is the exact wording:

> Congress shall make **no law** respecting an establishment of religion, or prohibiting the free exercise thereof; **or abridging the freedom of speech**, or of the press; or the right of the people peaceably to assemble, and to petition the Government for a redress of grievances.[37]

How could these lower courts have made a ruling contrary to this? This type of activity by liberal activist judges is very dangerous, and highlights the importance of keeping the Supreme Court in the conservative camp. The problem is that liberal thought is that abridging freedom of speech by taking away the opportunity to spend money on political advertising is that they always think that big government will help to solve the problem of having an unequal voice. Concerning laws restricting freedom of religion, there have been many such laws established; laws which are mostly

---

[37] The First Amendment to the Constitution of the United States of America

targeting Christians in direct violation of the constitution.

This is the opposite view that President Ronald Reagan had when he made his famous statement in his first inaugural address in 1981: "In this present crisis, government is **NOT** the solution to our problem; government **IS** the problem." He was right. The government is **STILL** the problem. Although the government is bigger than it was in the Reagan years, the actual size of the government has not grown as a portion of the population, there is still a lot of fat in government. And the more socialistic the government is, the bigger the government is. Notice the information below from a few years ago:

The percentage of public employees in the workforces of these countries ranges from 6.35 percent in Singapore to 33.87 percent in Sweden. Indeed the three lowest countries, and the only ones with fewer than 10 percent public employees, are Japan, Singapore, and Taiwan. The highest countries after Sweden are Denmark (32.3 percent) and Norway (29.25 percent). The remaining Scandinavian country, Finland, is fifth with 26.31 percent. In fourth place, just below Denmark, is Hungary. The other countries with public-employee percentages above 20 percent are

Greece (22.3 percent), Canada, and Poland, Greece being the lowest in this group of eight countries, despite all the negative attention its public-employee workforce has received lately.

The rest of the countries in my list (that is excluding the above-20 percent and below-10 percent countries), are grouped pretty tightly between about 12 and 19 percent. The United States is in approximately the middle, with 16.42 percent. Surprisingly, it is well ahead of Israel, Spain, Italy, Germany, France, and Portugal. The European countries with the lowest percentage of public workers are the Netherlands and Austria, but Portugal is only slightly above the Netherlands.[38]

Make no mistake about it, the leftist liberals want to grow the government to the level of what is seen in Sweden, which as a percentage of the population is twice as large as ours. In fact this is the chant of the Left....bigger government. If you will recall, President Obama stated a few years ago that these people who think they built a business

---

[38] http://www.becker-posner-blog.com/2011/09/too-many-government-workersposner.html

from scratch on their own were wrong. He said something to the effect of: "You didn't do that! The Government did that for you." From this statement, it is obvious that he has never built a business before.

Having gone through this process on a number of occasions myself, there is not even one iota of truth to this statement. In order to build a business, you must be willing to dedicate yourself to it. It usually takes long hours and hard work. Most of the time, the first, second, or third time you try, you will fail. But in order to be successful you must be diligent and willing to do what it takes, many times making huge sacrifices in your personal life in order to make it. So why would he say such a thing. When I built a business with my family years ago, there was absolutely NOTHING that the government did to help us. But this is the Leftist mindset!

## Freedom of the Press

If you have ever been to an amusement park, you probably have been to a place in the park called the fun house. In there they have several mirrors that are deliberately designed to distort your image. It really is funny to go in there and see the different ways that it distorts your body and you will laugh a lot. Today the mainstream media does something similar with much of what they term as news and there is nothing funny about it. They are creating distorted news every single day.

For example during the 2016 Presidential campaign, the negative media coverage of Donald Trump was 77% according to a study released in December of 2016 by the Harvard Kennedy School's Shorenstein Center on Media, Politics and Public Policy.[39] Also, during the first month of President Trump's administration, it was reported that the three major national news networks dedicated 54 percent of their time, or 16 hours, reporting on the president and his staff. Of that reporting, 88 percent of it was negative.[40]

As we could see from the quotation of the first amendment above, the Constitution also requires freedom of the press. But this is definitely not a problem today. The problem with the press today is that the press, in the form of the mainstream media, has drifted so far from actual news reporting that much of it has become propaganda. From the mainstream media we find that much of the news we get is "fun house" news. It is a distortion of the truth. President Trump has called

---

[39] http://www.newsmax.com/Newsfront/negative-media-coverage-donald-trump-hillary-clinton/2016/12/07/id/762783/
[40] http://www.newsmax.com/Newsfront/Nightly-News-Coverage-Trump-Negative/2017/03/02/id/776553/

the media out and told many of them that they are "fake news."

It is absolutely possible to create a set of mirrors that will mislead you and will flatter you. But is this what you really want to see?

In a book entitled "*LEFT TURN How liberal media bias distorts the American Mind*," author Tim Groseclose exposes this bias. Although it was written in 2011, Groseclose points out in the first paragraph of the Preface that in a typical presidential election, the Washington correspondents vote about 93-7 for the Democrat, while the rest of the country comes closer to 50-50. But this is having a profound effect on the thinking of the people because this is the news source of most Americans.

In his book, there is a test that is designed to determine your PQ, or your political quotient. This means it tells you whether you are conservative, liberal or centrist in your political views. How does it do this? By comparing your votes on specific bills as compared to how the US Congress and Senate voted on previous bills voted on by these entities. The range is 0 – 100, with 0 being fully conservative, and 100 being fully liberal. I took the test, and my score was in the area of 15-20, which shows I have a strong conservative bias.

So your political bias all depends on where you get your news source and what your criteria for judging is in these news sources. Note what Groseclose says about this:

> People often mistake bias, relative to other media outlets, as an absolute bias. That is, for instance, Fox News is clearly more conservative than ABC, CBS, CNN, NBC, and National Public Radio. Some will conclude that "therefore, this means that Fox News has a conservative bias." But this says nothing about its bias on any absolute scale. Instead, maybe it is centrist, and possibly even left-leaning, while all the others are far left. It is like concluding that six-three is short just because it is short compared to professional basketball players.

> The point illustrates a common misconception about the Drudge Report. According to my analysis, the Drudge Report is approximately the most fair, balanced, and centrist news outlet in the United States. Yet, the overwhelming majority of media commentators claim that it has a conservative bias. The problem, I believe, is that such commentators mistake relative bias for absolute bias. Yes, the Drudge Report is more conservative than the average U.S.

news outlet. But it is a logical mistake to use that to infer that it is biased on an absolute scale.

The same is true, I believe, with ABC News anchor Charles Gibson. He is nothing but fair and centrist in my judgment. In fact, one of the methods that I document finds that ABC's Good Morning America, during his tenure, was approximately the most unbiased of all U.S. media outlets. In my view, he was willing to ask tough questions, equally, to the two candidates during the 2008 election. However, because he directed more tough questions to Barack Obama than most of the other mainstream outlets did, he was charged with a conservative bias. Here again, such a claim mistakes relative bias with absolute bias.[41]

Many Americans have considered The New York Times to be a scholarly and reputable news source. But we are seeing more and more evidence of its **drastic turn to the left** to the point that **it is actually becoming a propaganda source in**

---

[41] Groseclose PhD, Tim. Left Turn: How Liberal Media Bias Distorts the American Mind (Kindle Locations 534-547). St. Martin's Press. Kindle Edition.

**Left wing Politics.** Having taken the test Groseclose has issued, it is easy to spot which direction these News sources lean, and it is clear that The New York Times is now leaning far to the liberal side of the spectrum. They will even admit it. Note what was stated on July 25, 2004 by Daniel Okrent. The public editor of The New York Times, wrote an article entitled "Is the New York Times a Liberal Newspaper?" It began:

> Of course it is. The fattest file on my hard drive is jammed with letters from the disappointed, the dismayed and the irate who find in this newspaper a liberal bias that infects not just political coverage but a range of issues from abortion to zoology to the appointment of an admitted Democrat to be its watchdog. (That would be me.) ... I'll get to the politics-and-policy issues this fall (I want to watch the campaign coverage before I conclude anything), but for now my concern is the flammable stuff that ignites the right. These are the social issues; gay rights, gun control, abortion and environmental regulation, among others.

And if you think The Times plays it down the middle on any of them, you've been reading the paper with your eyes closed.[42]

We find much of the same with the Washington Post. Note the following quote by Deborah Howell:

Some of the conservatives' complaints about a liberal tilt are valid. Journalism naturally draws liberals; we like to change the world. I'll bet that most Post journalists voted for Obama. I did. There are centrists at the Post as well. But the conservatives I know here feel so outnumbered that they don't even want to be quoted by name in a memo.[43]

CBS News also has admitted this in the past:

Andrew Heyward, the former president of CBS News, made a similar admission to then CBS reporter Bernard Goldberg:

---

[42] Groseclose PhD, Tim. Left Turn: How Liberal Media Bias Distorts the American Mind (Kindle Locations 813-819). St. Martin's Press. Kindle Edition. This was taken from:
http://www.nytimes.com/2004/07/25/opinion/the-public-editor-is-the-new-york-times-a-liberal-newspaper.html?_r=0

[43] Ibid. (Kindle Locations 2501-2505). St. Martin's Press. Kindle Edition. Taken from Deborah Howell, "Remedying the Bias Perception," Washington Post, November 16, 2008, p. B06.

Look Bernie, of course there's a liberal bias in the news. All the networks tilt left. Come on, we all know it— the whole damn world knows it— but that doesn't mean we have to put it on the air![44]

Then there is the Case of CNN, another Leftist news organization. The head of CNN even recently admitted it in an interview with the Wall Street Journal. He said:

"I think it was a legitimate criticism of CNN that it was a little too liberal."[45]

But that is a huge understatement. The facts show otherwise. I believe it is now a far left leaning political propagandist organization. Why do I say that? They have an avowed communist as an often used political commentator. This often is used to represent their views.

Politifact, a left leaning news outlet notes Van Jones was an avowed communist. Jones was arrested in 1992 during a protest of the acquittal of the police officers accused of beating Rodney King

---

[44] Groseclose PhD, Tim. Left Turn: How Liberal Media Bias Distorts the American Mind (Kindle Locations 821-824). St. Martin's Press. Kindle Edition.

[45] Ibid., also www.wsj.com/articles/cnn-enjoys-outsize-ratings-boost-from-presidential-race-1462126349

but later released. Note the following taken from the Politifact website:

> Although the charges were dropped, Jones said that while in jail, "I met all these young radical people of color – I mean really radical, communists and anarchists. And it was like 'This is what I need to be a part of.' I spent the next 10 years of my life working with a lot of those people I met in jail, trying to be a revolutionary."

> "In the months that followed," the Express article said, "he let go of any lingering thoughts that he might fit in with the status quo. 'I was a rowdy nationalist on April 28th, and then the verdicts came down on April 29th' he said. 'By August, I was a communist.'"[46]

It doesn't take long watching what they do and do not publish to understand this. Why would CNN place him in such a high position of favor on their network if this was not true?

Conservative talk show host Michael Savage points out in his book "The Savage Nation" that CNN was actually revealing information to our enemy

---

[46] http://www.politifact.com/truth-o-meter/statements/2009/sep/08/glenn-beck/glenn-beck-says-van-jones-avowed-communist/

during military exercises. He pointed out that the terrorists often tune in to these revealing news posts. He's right about this! If you have watched CNN in times of war, you would see that their news correspondents are giving away too much information.

So there you have it. In some of these news outlets, there is not even the pretense of them publishing the real truth. And since that time, there is considerable evidence that it has gotten even worse in its reporting bias. It adds credibility to those now calling it "Fake News."

It has been reported and I have noticed that many of the anchors on the Fox News channel seem to have no problem revealing their political party affiliation. Many have claimed to be Independent also. But some, like Sean Hannity claim to be conservative. However, if someone asks the main network news Anchors what their party affiliations are, they act as if they are offended. Couldn't they at least state specifically that they are either conservative or liberal? Then at least there would be somewhat of a filter to help those listeners understand the nature of their bias.

There is a way to remedy this but it must begin in our schools. Young minds are so very impressionable. The conservatives are losing this battle right now, but it is my hope that the Trump administration will last eight years to give the conservatives time to counter all of the damage done by the Obama administration. It appears that he is making inroads into this problem because he has no desire to be politically correct, and calls out the media. Maybe people will wake up to the fact that here is a man who tells it like it is, and truly loves his country. He has even refused to accept pay for the many hours every day that he tirelessly works to "Make America Great Again." God knows we need all the help we can get.

**Second Amendment Rights**

The second amendment to the constitution states the following:

> A well-regulated Militia, being necessary to the security of a free State, **the right of the people to keep and bear Arms, shall not be infringed**.[47]

There is nothing unclear about this. The people's right to bear arms is a right protected by the Constitution of the United States. Not only is it protected, it clearly states that this right **shall not**

---

[47] The Second Amendment to the Constitution of the United States of America

**be infringed.** There is no stronger language in the constitution than this.

There has always been a running dialog in this country about whether or not the second amendment is a good thing. The liberals on the left claim that all guns should be banned and everything would be better. The conservatives on the right believe that this constitutional amendment is one of the stalwarts of individual liberty.

But never has this dispute heated up any more than it did on December 14, 2012. On this date 20 year old Adam Lanza brutally murdered his mother with four gunshots to the head. Then he proceeded to take her Bushmaster carbine rifle along with some other guns and go to the Sandy Hook elementary school. There he went on a killing spree that included 20 children between the age of six and seven years old and six adult staff members.

When it became clear that he was pinned in, he turned one of his guns on himself and was found dead with a gunshot wound to his head with another of the guns he was carrying. Earlier that same year in a movie theater in Aurora Colorado a mass shooting occurred in which 12 people were killed and 70 injured.

After the massacre at the Sandy Hook school the liberals put on a full assault to create more gun control. Gun control advocacy groups pressed as almost never before to continue in their efforts to destroy the second amendment. But a very simple question to ask is this: **Is the gun to blame for these killings?**

During the Obama administration, gun sales exploded. In fact it has been reported that the background checks required to buy a gun more than doubled between 2008 and 2016. This was even more pronounced just prior to the 2016 election. Why did this happen? Perhaps because of the continual threat that was in the background in the mind of the public that there might be changes in the gun control laws that would make gun ownership more difficult.

But behind all of this, there must be the realization that a gun is a tool...nothing more and nothing less. It can be used for good or bad just like any tool. What about knives? If someone uses a knife to kill, is it the knife's fault? What about trucks? When a truck is used to drive headlong into a crowd and purposely kill 84 people like what recently happened in Nice France? Is it the fault of the truck? What about a pressure cooker? Should a pressure cooker be banned because someone used it as a bomb to kill and maim a bunch of people at the Boston Marathon? The same could be said of pipes used to make pipe bombs, or fertilizer used to make bombs. To blame the tool is preposterous!

Because the liberal media is committed to protecting these ideas so strongly, seldom are the good effects of the second amendment ever reported by the main-stream media. One of the most idiotic ideas ever orchestrated is the idea of gun free zones. The Sandy Hook school was a **gun free zone** as required by federal law! Yes, that's right. The Gun Free School Zone Act of 1990 prohibits anyone from having a gun within a school zone. Could this have been a reason why Adam Lanza went to Sandy Hook and killed all these kids and teachers? When a gun free zone is in place does anyone really think that a criminal is going to abide by that directive?

I believe the Gun Free School Zone Act of 1990 is **unconstitutional.** As far as that goes, I believe **that ALL** gun free zones are unconstitutional. There is no question that this violates the language of the second amendment which states that **the right of the people to keep and bear Arms, shall NOT be infringed**. Gun free zones are meant to infringe the legal rights of those who **have already been heavily screened** by the government and found to be free of any issues that would cause them not to be trusted with a gun.

On June 12, 2016, in a horrific act of violence 49 people were killed by a heavily armed Islamic jihadist gunman at the Pulse nightclub. Could it be that this incident could have been greatly diminished if the right of those who entered this nightclub as responsible heavily screened concealed-carry permit holders were allowed to keep their gun concealed with them in the club?

This is a question worth considering.

Especially vulnerable to attack by criminals are women. This is because most violent criminal acts are done by men, and many of these such as rape and assault are against women. With the increase in publicity of gun ownership, there has been a sharp increase in women buying guns for self-protection. This has been proven to be a good thing. Notice this incident:

> Police said a Georgia mother hiding with her children shot an intruder five times after he chased them in their own home Friday afternoon, CBS affiliate WGCL-TV reports.

> Authorities said the woman took her twin 9-year-old children to the attic as the man broke into their house with a crowbar. He reportedly busted open the front door and gave chase when he heard the woman call out to her children.

Investigators said the man chased the family into a crawl space near the attic, and when he opened a door the mother opened fire, striking him five times. He then stumbled out of the house, got into a car and crashed into a tree line in an attempt to flee from the scene.

The woman and her children then ran to a neighbor's home for help, WGCL-TV reports.

Investigators said 32-year-old Paul Slater is in critical condition and in an intensive care unit at Gwinnett Medical Center.

He reportedly has an extensive criminal history.[48]

When Donald Trump, a pro-Second Amendment candidate won the election most people, myself included, thought that gun sales would drop. But that has not been the case. Yet, gun sales from election day in November through the first quarter of 2017 are still climbing.

---

[48] http://www.cbsnews.com/news/georgia-mother-hides-children-shoots-intruder-5-times-during-home-invasion-police-say/

Fox News reports the following with regard to gun sales:

> The National African-American Gun Association saw a 7% increase in members just over the Thanksgiving weekend. NBC News contacted gun storeowners who reported seeing up to four times as many black and minority customers. The Liberal Gun Club says that its membership is up 10%. Many news stories quote liberals saying that they bought a gun for the first time after the election.
>
> There were other signs that gun control was losing popularity. "Miss Sloane," is a pro-gun control movie that flopped miserably in December. Despite being heavily advertised and promoted in the mainstream media, the film's second weekend saw an average of fewer than 10 viewers per day per movie theater.[49]

Perhaps it was a fear of the Trump Presidency, but as Fox News continued to report, perhaps there may be evidence that liberals are beginning to

---

[49] http://www.foxnews.com/opinion/2017/03/13/in-2017-women-and-minorities-are-buying-guns-heres-why.html

change their views on guns. Note again the Fox News report:

> Among the seven states (plus the District of Columbia) that the New York Times categorizes as consistently voting for Democrats, there was a 20.6% increase in background checks from October to November. By contrast, there was only a 4.5% increase among the 19 states that the Times labeled as consistently Republican.
>
> Excluding California, there was still a 13.1% increase in gun sales in the other heavily Democrat states and DC. This was still almost 3 times the increase in heavily Republican states.[50]

Although the report indicated that gun sales were down in California, it showed background checks increased for both heavily Democratic and Republican states. Fox reported that the trend in gun ownership is continuing to increase. For example, concealed handgun permits have soared from about 4.6 million in 2007 to 14.5 million in 2016. Fifty-seven percent of Americans now believe that gun ownership "protects people from

---

[50] Ibid.

becoming victims of crime. Without a doubt there has been a major shift in the attitude of blacks and women. Both of these groups are now purchasing guns in larger numbers than ever before.

As I conclude this chapter, and from the information we see above, it is clear that these constitutional amendments must be preserved! The framers of the Constitution knew what they were doing with the creation of the first and second amendment.

There is so much more to say, but with this, I rest my case against liberalism. It is the scourge of our nation and a tragedy of hate against those who built a nation described as "One nation under God with liberty and justice for all."

# One Nation under God

**But are we really?**
**Why has Godlessness increased?**
**Is there PROOF that there is a God?**
**Is it the same God as the God of Islam?**
**How can we be sure we can trust in God?**

The Pledge of Allegiance to the flag of the United States of America was originally created in 1887 by Colonel George Balch, an Admiral in the US Navy. But it did not survive its original form which was as follows:

"We give our heads and hearts to God and our country; one country, one language, one flag!"

It was revised five years later by Francis Bellamy

and read:

> "I pledge allegiance to my Flag and the Republic for which it stands, one nation, indivisible, with liberty and justice for all."

The next revision came in 1923, a revision which stood for just over 30 years. It read as follows:

> "I pledge allegiance to the flag of the United States of America, and to the Republic for which it stands, one Nation indivisible, with liberty and justice for all."

The final version was changed in 1954 by an act of Congress. There is a good unbiased history of this in Wikipedia. It tells us how President Eisenhower was in a Church service in which his Pastor George MacPherson Docherty gave a sermon based on the Gettysburg Address entitled "A New Birth of Freedom." The Pastor argued that the strength of the nation was **not due to its arms** but rather **in its spirit and higher purpose**, but that there was **something missing** in the pledge, and that was as Lincoln himself declared; that we are separated from other nations by the fact that we are a nation "**under God**." This was a great inspiration to the President and caused him to take action. Wikipedia states:

President Eisenhower had been baptized a Presbyterian very recently, just a year before. He responded enthusiastically to Docherty in a conversation following the service. Eisenhower acted on his suggestion the next day and on February 8, 1954, Rep. Charles Oakman (R-Mich.), introduced a bill to that effect. Congress passed the necessary legislation and Eisenhower signed the bill into law on Flag Day, June 14, 1954. Eisenhower stated:

"From this day forward, the millions of our school children will daily proclaim in every city and town, every village and rural school house, the dedication of our nation and our people to the Almighty.... In this way we are reaffirming the transcendence of religious faith in America's heritage and future; in this way we shall constantly strengthen those spiritual weapons which forever will be our country's most powerful resource, in peace or in war."

The phrase "under God" was incorporated into the Pledge of Allegiance on June 14, 1954, by a Joint Resolution of Congress amending § 4 of the Flag Code enacted in 1942[51]

Here is the 1954 version of the Pledge of Allegiance to the flag, which is still current today:

I pledge allegiance to the Flag of the United States of America, and to the Republic for which it stands, one Nation under God, indivisible, with liberty and justice for all."

I believe that this was a momentous event in our nation's history. Why? Because it had been 178 years since the Declaration of Independence and here was a President who realized the importance of this truth. Being one nation, **the reason** we **were** indivisible, with liberty and justice for all, was that **we were** one nation **under God**. It was **because of trust in God** that the United States of America was so blessed.

Jesus said: "Every kingdom divided against itself is laid waste, and no city or house divided against itself will stand." Matthew 12:25 (ESV)

---

But since Ike made this momentous speech, and this was added to the pledge of allegiance, we as a nation have drifted badly. In fact, we in this nation are now more divided than at any time since the Civil War. The Conservatives say the Constitution should be interpreted as the framers intended to **preserve** Judeo-Christian values. The Progressive Liberals proclaim that the Constitution needs to be a living document that needs to be changed to fit our **changing** values and customs.

This conflict of ideals has reached a boiling point. The framers declared "In God we Trust." The Liberals today proclaim that putting God in anything is a **violation** of the First Amendment. The Conservatives say putting God in everything is an **expression** of the First Amendment. The rift between these factions is getting deeper every day. So the big question we need to ask now is: Can we survive as a nation?

Even if you have proclaimed yourself to be Godless, you have to realize that history bears out the words Jesus spoke centuries ago. Even **Abraham Lincoln himself realized this**. In his failed bid for the Senate seat of Illinois in 1858, in a speech that would nonetheless mark his career, he said:

> "A house divided against itself cannot stand."
> I believe this government cannot endure, permanently half slave and half free. I do not

> expect the Union to be dissolved — I do not
> expect the house to fall — but I do expect it
> will cease to be divided. It will become all one
> thing or all the other."

Lincoln was quoting Jesus in the first part of this statement. There was plenty of history behind Jesus' statement. Every time the nation of Israel left God, God left Israel and the result was disastrous. Lincoln knew that history supported him in that claim. The Roman empire rotted from the inside out due to its decayed base of morality. Alexander the Great's empire failed after his death due to rivalries of those who succeeded him.

As I have shown in the pages of this book, we in the USA are facing a similar and very troubling dilemma. I believe our nation has **never been more divided** than this since Lincoln's time. I also believe that this is in some ways similar to Lincoln's day. The division is Conservative vs. Liberal; Godly vs Godless; and finally, Tolerance vs Intolerance. So the big question is: Is this reversible? Is there any way to become united again?

## One Nation under God: Is this the right label?

Due to the rise of Liberalism in this country, our institutions of higher learning have become institutions of Godless thought. We covered much of this in an earlier chapter. It is definitely not "in vogue" to believe in God. As we observed in a previous chapter, most institutions of higher learning are liberal.

According to a Gallop poll released in 2014, 42% of Americans believe in Creation by God, 31% of Americans believe that God guided evolution, and 19% of Americans are Atheists.[52]

The good part is that despite all of the liberalism taught in colleges which push the theory of a Godless Evolution, the trend of people who believe in Creation since 1982 remains steady at just over 42%. The downside is that the trend of atheists has risen from 9 to 19% during that time, **but the majority of people DO believe in God!**

Yes, when you total up those who believe in Creation by God and Evolution assisted by God, the total of all people is 74%. This was confirmed by a Rasmussen poll in 2015, where 3⁄4 of all Americans say that Religion played an important part in their life.[53]

---

52

http://www.patheos.com/blogs/friendlyatheist/2014/06/02/gallup-poll-42-of-americans-are-creationists/

53

http://www.rasmussenreports.com/public_content/videos/2015_02/what_america_thinks_in_god_we_trust

Now I have to say that I am surprised at that considering the fact that Liberal values always seem to lead to the **denial of God**. But this does not answer a very crucial question, and that question is: Do we Trust in God?

First of all, what about those who do not believe in God? I am troubled by the fact that the Gallup poll stated that Atheism rose from 9% in 1982 to 19% in 2014. For those who do not believe in God, let's consider a few facts:

- The universe is so large that scientists estimate that it would take between 2 and 5 billion lifetimes to take a tour at the speed of light! Yet it is so small that it would take the whole population of the earth 90 million years to count the atoms in a cup of water.

- If you could put all of your DNA molecules end to end, the DNA would reach from the Earth to the Sun and back over 600 times. Keep in mind that the sun is over 92 million miles away.

- The chances of "The Big Bang" creating all of the order in the Universe including life without God behind it is about the same as an explosion in a print shop creating a printed dictionary.

- Each cell in the human body contains more information than in the dictionaries of the top 10 languages on earth combined.

- Scientists have found that Mitochondrial DNA only allows for the transmission of that DNA to the same species. This disallows the possibility of man evolving from the lower forms of life.

Large volumes have been written to prove the facts that I have listed above. But my question to you atheists is this: With these facts in mind, **do you really believe** that there was no intelligent design behind all of the order of the universe?

One of the things that many people use to try to disprove that God exists is the problem of pain. Yes, this is a complex problem, and the answers are also complex. Christian philosopher C.S. Lewis wrote a book on it called *The Problem of Pain*, in which he Chronicles the reasons why the problem of pain is necessary. The answer to the problem from his perspective is that in order for humans to truly have free will, it means that some of the choices we make will be disastrous. If God would intervene, then there would be no free will. Thus in effect, we would be reduced to puppets in a staged game.

In his book, "The Case for Faith" Author Lee Strobel who was at one time a conformed Atheist, journals his journey to faith in God. In his first objection to God he chronicles his discussion on this subject with Peter Kreeft Ph. D a philosophy professor at Villanova University. In contrast to many professors whose answers are relatively boring, Strobel points out the fact that he got real world answers from this learned professor.

Strobel described to him an incident that was related to him by a Christian named Charles Templeton, who was suddenly converted to Atheism by simply looking at a picture from *Life Magazine* of a mother holding a child who had just died because of a lack of rain. It was Templeton's belief that this disproves that there is a loving God. His question was something to this effect: "How is it possible that God would allow such a thing to a precious child when all he had to do was make it rain? To him this was proof that God does not exist.

In response to this, Kreeft gave an illustration that was very thought provoking. Here is an excerpt from the conversation written by Strobel:

Kreeft thought for a moment. "Look at it this way," he said. "Would you agree that the difference between us and God is greater than the difference between us and, say, a bear?"

I nodded.

"Okay, then, imagine a bear trap and a hunter who, out of sympathy, wants to liberate him. He tries to win the bear's confidence, but he can't do it, so he has to shoot the bear full of drugs. The bear, however, thinks this is an attack and that the hunter is trying to kill him. He doesn't realize that this is being done out of compassion."

"Then in order to get the bear out of the trap, the hunter has to push him further into the trap to release the tension on the spring. If the bear were semiconscious at that point, he would be more convinced that the hunter was trying to cause him suffering and pain. But the bear would be wrong. He reaches this incorrect conclusion because he's not a human being."

Kreeft let this illustration soak in for a moment. "Now," he concluded, "how can anyone be certain that's not an analogy between us and God? I believe God does the same to us sometimes, and we can't comprehend why he does it any more than the bear can understand the motivations of the hunter. As the bear could have trusted the hunter, **so we can trust God**."[54] (emphasis mine)

Do you want statistical evidence? I pointed out one incidence in an earlier chapter to make my case, but let's look at another one. This is taken from a book by Dr. John Ankerberg, Dr. John Weldon, Dr. Walter Kaiser (Excerpted from their book *The Case for Jesus the Messiah*.)

Professor Emeritus of Science at Westmont College, Peter Stoner, has calculated the probability of one man fulfilling the major prophecies made concerning the Messiah. The estimates were worked out by twelve different classes of 600 college students.

For example, concerning Micah 5:2, where it states the Messiah would be born in Bethlehem Ephrathah, Stoner and his students determined the average population of Bethlehem from the time of Micah to the present; then they divided it by the average

[54] Strobel, Lee, The Case For Faith, A journalist Investigates the Toughest Objections to Christianity, Copyright 2000 Zondervan, pp 42-44.

population of the earth during the same period. They concluded that the chance of one man being born in Bethlehem was one in $2.8 \times 10^5$ –or rounded, one in 300,000. After examining eight different prophecies, they conservatively estimated that the chance of one man fulfilling all eight prophecies was one in $10^{17}$. To illustrate how large the number $10^{17}$ is (a figure with 17 zeros), Stoner gave this illustration.

Imagine covering the entire state of Texas with silver dollars to a level of two feet deep. The total number of silver dollars needed to cover the whole state would be $10^{17}$. Now, choose just one of those silver dollars, mark it and drop it from an airplane. Then thoroughly stir all the silver dollars all over the state. When that has been done, blindfold one man, tell him he can travel wherever he wishes in the state of Texas. But sometime he must stop, reach down into the two feet of silver dollars and try to pull up that one specific silver dollar that has been marked. Now, the chance of his finding that one silver dollar in the state of Texas would be the chance the prophets had for eight of their prophecies coming true in any one man in the future.[55]

WOW! You have to be impressed by these statistics. This leaves no possibility for error. You **can argue with ideas**, but you **cannot argue with facts**. This is more scientific proof that **we can trust God!**

I realize that this is a very short list of proofs that God exists, and for that matter proof that here was a Messiah who came to this earth and died for us. But this was the belief of the founding fathers of this nation. I firmly believe this **has answered the question:** Is this the right label? **We are unequivocally** one nation under God. But there are more questions to be answered.

## Do we want to be one nation under God?

It is truly up to the next generation of Americans as to whether we will continue into be what we have been in our past. Before becoming President, Barrack Obama, said in a speech on June 28, 2006

Whatever we once were, we are no longer a Christian nation – at least, not just. We are

---

[55] By Dr. John Ankerberg, Dr. John Weldon, Dr. Walter Kaiser (Excerpted from their book *The Case for Jesus the Messiah.*) 2014 ATRi Publishing. Look at case #13 Micah 5:2.

also a Jewish nation, a Muslim nation, a Buddhist nation, and a Hindu nation, and a nation of nonbelievers.

In 2009 in a Press Conference in the nation of Turkey, President Obama stated:

> One of the great strengths of the United States, is ... we have a very large Christian population — we do not consider ourselves a Christian nation or a Jewish nation or a Muslim nation. We consider ourselves a nation of citizens who are bound by ideals and a set of values.[56]

Although Barrack Obama has professed to be a Christian himself, I have to wonder why Obama would make such a statement which is radically opposed to what we see and have shown to be in the founding documents of our country. Does what he said sound like something a Christian would say considering what we know about the inscriptions on the buildings in Washington D.C.? For example, has Barrack Obama ever read the prayer of George Washington for this nation? After reading it, and knowing that Washington put his life on the line for these ideals, could any leader of

---

[56] http://www.huffingtonpost.com/2009/04/06/obama-us-not-a-christian_n_183772.html

this country possibly say such a thing? Here is the prayer:

George Washington's Prayer for America

> **Almighty GOD**; we make our earnest prayer that Thou wilt keep the United States in Thy holy protection, that thou wilt incline the hearts of the citizens to cultivate a spirit of subordination and obedience to government; and entertain a brotherly affection and love for one another and for their fellow citizens of the United States of America at large. And finally that Thou wilt most graciously be pleased to dispose us all to do justice, to love mercy and to demean ourselves with that charity, humility and pacific temper of mind which were the characteristics of The Divine Author of our blessed religion, and without whose example in these things we can never hope to be a happy nation. Grant our supplication, we beseech thee, **through Jesus Christ Our Lord**. Amen[57] (emphasis mine)

---

[57]

http://fourwinds10.com/siterun_data/spiritual/prayer/news.php?q=1316443487

What about Thomas Jefferson? Did Barrack Obama know this about President Jefferson? During his presidency Jefferson frequently negotiated with Indian tribes and he even created a little book called ***Philosophy of Jesus*** that was made up of cut and pasted Bible verses that he used as a primer to teach the Indians about Jesus. He even believed that Christian missionaries to the Indians was so important that **he provided the missionaries at government expense**. That little book is called the ***Jefferson Bible*** by revisionist historians.[58] (emphasis mine)

Did Barrack Obama know that President John Quincy Adams said this?

"My hopes of a future life are all **founded upon the Gospel of Christ** and I cannot cavil or quibble away [evade or object to]. . . . the whole tenor of His conduct by which He sometimes positively asserted and at others countenances [permits] His disciples in asserting that He was God."

---

[58] http://www.whatchristianswanttoknow.com/christian-presidents-10-leaders-known-for-their-faith/#ixzz4cccNN3Um

"In the chain of human events, the birthday of the nation is indissolubly linked with the birthday of **the Savior**. The Declaration of Independence **laid the cornerstone of human government upon the first precepts of Christianity**."[59] (emphasis mine)

These websites listed below would have provided him with these truth's which would have been appropriate for him to quote. There are many more such quotes from our past leaders that we could quote. But regarding the statement that President Obama stated, we must ask: Why would he rather make a statement such as this, which is pure propaganda with absolutely no consideration for the truth of our nation's history, which is that we **ARE** a Christian nation?

The reason is simple. When he was elected to the office of the Presidency, many people were hoping that he, as the first African American President, would keep his word and use his power to heal the wounds of this divided nation. But history has shown that this was not his goal. This was shown by how when racial incidents occurred he incited

---

[59] Ibid.

violence in the black community instead of quelling the violence. Two such incidents, such as in the killing of Travon Martin, and the killing of Michael Brown by Police spawned such violence that soon there became an all-out war on our Police departments in much of America.

Where was President Obama when the murder rate in his own home town of Chicago was rising? Why did he not take drastic action to stop all of this violence, much of which was black on black violence? It was because such a thing did not fit his political agenda.

His goal was to **change America to his radical Leftist Ideology** and in this **he succeeded.** He did make massive inroads especially in the minds and hearts of our most treasured possession, our young people. The result has been that we are more deeply divided as a nation than ever before. Is there anything we can do to reverse this, and return to our roots?

## The Rise of Islam

President Obama has been right in one sense. Due to his political agenda, this nation has drifted even more **radically to the left**. Over the last 60 years we have moved from a nation whose values were Christian to a nation where Christians are discriminated against; a nation where Christian values were respected and honored to a nation where people of faith are considered to be lower class and less educated. The News media is more of a propaganda arm of the left than a true proponent of unbiased news.

This radical move to the left has gotten to the point where there are **radical Islamic Jihadists** living among us in increasing numbers. We have seen such moves in other nations of the world in even greater number. The rise of Islam in these nations has brought with it no peace. It **has brought** a big increase in radical jihadism. People are being slaughtered in the streets by terrorists, who purposely kill innocent people because of their faith. Why is this so? Because unlike what they claim, **Islam is not a religion of peace**. Islam is a religion which is based on the Quran. The Quran in no uncertain terms **requires the adherents to take the world by force** and overthrow the opposition by violent means.

In an article entitled "What makes Islam so different" we find the following about this "religion of peace:"

The Quran contains **at least 109 verses that call Muslims to war** with nonbelievers for the sake of Islamic rule.

Some are quite graphic, with commands to chop off heads and fingers and kill infidels wherever they may be hiding. Muslims who do not join the fight are called 'hypocrites' and warned that Allah will send them to Hell if they do not join the slaughter.

(Author's note: From this article as referenced below, here are just a couple of them.)

Quran (2:191-193) – *"And* **kill them wherever you find them***, and turn them out from where they have turned you out. And Al-Fitnah* [disbelief or unrest] *is worse than killing… but if they desist, then lo! Allah is forgiving and merciful. And fight them until there is no more Fitnah* [disbelief and worshipping of others along with Allah] *and worship is for Allah alone.*

Quran (4:95) – *"Not equal are those of the believers who sit (at home), except those who are disabled (by injury or are blind or lame, etc.), and those who strive hard and fight in the Cause of Allah with their wealth and their lives. Allah has preferred in grades those who strive hard and fight with their wealth and their lives above those who sit (at home).Unto each, Allah has promised good (Paradise), but Allah has preferred those who strive hard and fight, above those who sit (at home) by a huge reward* "[60]

The last verse **criticizes** those who would not advocate violence. **Does this sound like a religion of peace?**

This religion poses a real threat to America, and is being ignored by all politicians. While it is true that most Muslim adherents have ignored these verses, and are peaceful, here is the problem. Out of the 7.5 Billion People on the planet today, approximately **1.2 Billion are Muslims**. Those who are **radical or have become radicalized** are somewhere around 20%.

If these figures are correct, that means that there are 240,000,000 (two hundred and forty million) radical Islamists on the earth today. These followers of Islam want to **carry out the mandates listed in the Quran** as we have noted above. They are the ones who want to **kill by any means** possible. They are the ones **who will behead people** just because they are not Muslims. That is an astounding number of people **who want to destroy Western civilization as**

---

**we know it!**

Let's contrast this with what the Bible says about Christianity. **Jesus himself** made the following proclamations:

> "You have heard that it was said, 'You shall love your neighbor and hate your enemy.' But I say to you, Love your enemies and pray for those who persecute you, so that you may be sons of your Father who is in heaven. For he makes his sun rise on the evil and on the good, and sends rain on the just and on the unjust. (Matthew 5:43-45 ESV)

> "But love your enemies, and do good, and lend, expecting nothing in return, and your reward will be great, and you will be sons of the Most High, for he is kind to the ungrateful and the evil." (Luke 6:35 ESV)

> "Greater love has no one than this, that someone lay down his life for his friends." (John 5:13)

Yes, this is the difference. Christianity espouses **love and peace**. Islam espouses **hate and violence**. Radical Islam **must be defeated**. But when we consider the words of the Quran, we must realize that within the Islamic faith there will always be the potential for extremism and violence. This is a problem with potentially dire consequences, not only for us, but for the entire civilized world.

## The God of Islam is NOT our God!

When the great leaders of this nation created our founding documents, it is important to realize that the phrase "One nation under God" was a reference to a God whose identity is revealed in the Bible. This was recorded by the Apostle Paul centuries ago when he said:

> "For the grace of God has appeared, bringing salvation for all people, training us to renounce ungodliness and worldly passions, and to live self-controlled, upright, and godly lives in the present age, waiting for our blessed hope, the appearing of the glory of **our great God and Savior Jesus Christ,** who gave himself for us to redeem us from all lawlessness and to purify for himself a people for his own possession who are zealous for good works. Declare these things; exhort and rebuke with all authority. Let no one disregard you." (Titus 2:11-15 ESV)

This is what the founders of our great nation meant when they said this is "One Nation under God." May it always be so.

# Epilogue

**"It is impossible to rightly govern a nation without God and the Bible."** — *George Washington*[61]

Christian Author, apologist, and philosopher C.S. Lewis noted in a chapter entitled *Human Pain* from his book, *The Problem of Pain,* the following:

> "The human spirit will not even begin to try to surrender self-will as long as all seems well with it. Now error and sin both have this property, that the deeper they are the less their victim suspects their existence; they are masked evil. Pain is unmasked, unmistakable

---

[61] http://www.great-quotes.com/quote/220058

evil; every man knows that something is wrong when he is being hurt."

Then later in the same chapter he makes a profound statement:

"God whispers to us in our pleasures, speaks in our conscience, but shouts in our pains: It is His megaphone to rouse a deaf world."[62]

As I write the closing words of this book, my precious daughter-in-law is lying in a hospital bed barley able to move. Her body and vitality were robbed by a disease that overtook her called meningitis, a disease that inflames the lining of the brain and spinal cord. With this, she had a seizure which apparently resulted in a stroke. Her vitals were devastated, her strength was lost, and now we are all praying for her recovery by the grace of God. **But we trust in God** for the outcome, whatever it may be. Why? Because we are told in his precious Word:

"And we know that for those who love God all things work together for good, for those who are called according to his purpose. ... ... Who shall separate us from the love of Christ? Shall tribulation, or distress, or

---

[62] Lewis, C.S. The Problem of Pain, MacMillan Paperbacks Edition 1962, Eleventh Printing, New York, N.Y., 1971. pages 92,93

persecution, or famine, or nakedness, or danger, or sword? As it is written, "For your sake we are being killed all the day long; we are regarded as sheep to be slaughtered." No, in all these things we are more than conquerors through him who loved us. For I am sure that neither death nor life, nor angels nor rulers, nor things present nor things to come, nor powers, nor height nor depth, nor anything else in all creation, will be able to separate us from the love of God in Christ Jesus our Lord." (Romans 8:28, 35-39 ESV)

We as Americans do not know what lies ahead for us. Therefore, if we want to make our lives meaningful, we must take action to counter the evils we face in this life. One thing is for sure, we will all suffer pain in this life, and we will all eventually die.

So what is our lot in life? If we are moral beings, we want our lives to count for something. As Americans, we want a life that is based on truth. We want our children to be taught truth. The great American Patriot, Patrick Henry, said:

It cannot be emphasized too strongly or too often that this great nation was founded, not by religionists; but by Christians, not on religions, but on the Gospel of Jesus Christ!"[63]

We, as did the early patriots who created the Republic in which we live, need to confront our challenge head on. Our challenge today which we have identified in this book is not from some distant Monarchy, or from an aggressive neighbor country who wants to take over our land and everything we own. Our challenge today comes from an opposition to the ideology proposed by Patrick Henry. That ideology is that which would seek to destroy the entire original reason for the establishment of the Constitution, and that was to give them freedom from the oppressive rule of excessive government; freedom of religion; and freedom of speech.

To get a sense of this, we must look at the reasons why the Pilgrims and Puritans set sail for America. They believed that they were acting in a similar manner to what the Bible outlines for the nation of Israel in the book of Exodus when they left the burdensome and oppressive rule of King Pharaoh of Egypt. Their ideal was to sail to America and establish for themselves a pure commonwealth which would be **of the people, by the people,**

---

[63] http://www.searchquotes.com/Patrick_Henry/Religion/quotes/

**and for the people, based on the principles of Christianity.**

## The Puritan Experiment

Under the leadership of John Winthrop, the Puritans sailed for the Americas about 10 years after the Pilgrims, somewhere around 1630. They knew the challenges they faced would be great, perhaps sometimes, even overwhelming. But they knew that at their very core, the very inner being of their souls was a strong faith, and in the New World, they would have the freedom to live their lives in accord with that expectation. They wanted a commonwealth that was purely and wholly Christian, and set out to establish such a government. The government would strictly adhere to the ideals of the Puritan faith which was based in the views of John Calvin. There was very little tolerance for those who wandered from the faith ideals set up at that time.

But the actual results of the experiment revealed a problem, **a flaw in their thinking**. With the establishment of a strictly religious society, they found that the very rules by which they were seeking to live **were also as oppressive** as the system from which they left, but in another sense. It was oppressive to those whose views differed from their own. Note the following from an article by PBS about this group:

John Winthrop understood that people were bound to disagree and was willing to tolerate a range of opinion and belief. But he also recognized that if dissent were not kept within bounds, it would undermine the community. And that is precisely what happened. Two members of the Massachusetts Bay Colony, <u>Roger Williams</u> and <u>Anne Hutchinson</u>, challenged the religious authority of the Puritan commonwealth and threatened to destroy Winthrop's vision of "a city upon a hill."

The colony survived, but over time its religious fervor diminished. Scholars disagree about when and why this happened. The Puritans themselves found it difficult to maintain a society in a state of creative uncertainty. In 1679, a Puritan synod met to deliberate the causes of widespread spiritual malaise. Blame was assigned to an increase in swearing; a tendency to sleep at sermons; the spread of sex and alcohol, especially in taverns, where women were known to bare their arms and, upon occasion, even their breasts; and, most telling, the marked increase in lying and lawsuits.[64]

This was later to be a lesson learned in the establishment of the constitution. If it was indeed to be of the people, by the people, and for the people, they needed to be able to exercise freedom of thought. Although the basis of their belief was Christianity, the Puritan experiment showed that the imposition of a strict set of rules would not work. People almost immediately rebelled.

## The Failed Socialism Experiment of the Pilgrims

In an earlier chapter, we spoke about the failed socialism experiment of the Pilgrims in the 1600s. Karl Marx, their social experiment was based on the same premise. That premise was:

"**From each** according to his ability, to each according to his needs"

As we stated earlier, these people signed a contract before they left England! They were as committed to making this work as anyone could be. They were Christians, true Christians who practiced the principles of Christian love sincerely. Remember that according to its provisions, each of the participants were required to pool all of their profits they got from the work that they did into a common pool, **no matter what their**

---

**profession, no matter how hard they worked, or what they did**. They were to take nothing out for themselves from their efforts, but **they would only take** from the common stock of goods what they needed to live. But despite all of these advantages, **the experiment was a disaster.** Within two years, **about half of the colonists died.** Why? Because there was no true incentive. It even broke down to the point where **people were stealing in order to survive**, which was one of the gravest sins of the Pilgrim community. Because of this lack of incentive, people automatically became lazy.

So as we recall from the earlier chapter, this experiment was so bad that the leadership abandoned this incentive killing system and moved to free market capitalism, and things immediately turned around for them. Everyone now had incentive to work and earn the fruits of their labor.

The results of this study were **absolutely profound**. They should be a **required study** for every student in America at some level, preferably early in high school.

**The Road back to Tyranny**

The **very big lesson** of the failed experiment of the Pilgrims in the 1600s was that at its core, **Socialism is a complete and utter failure**. In order for people to have a sense of self-worth, they must be free to work for themselves and enjoy the benefits of their work.

As we think about this failed experiment, we must look at the ideology behind this. Where today do we see this ideology portrayed? Where do we see the "spread the wealth" attitude prevalent today? Yes, you named it. **It is a major part of the Liberal Leftist Agenda.** But there is a difference. The Liberals want the socialist agenda to play out differently. The elitists want to be above it. They want to be the ruling class of it. It's OK for the masses to have this system that destroys the work ethic of the people. Then they can be subjects to a class of people that want to keep the ruling class structure the same.

This is the basis of Tyranny! The result of this type of government is always such as seen in the failed Pilgrim experiment. But on a larger scale, the effects are much worse. History has shown this to be true without a single exception. A socialistic society **always deteriorates** to the point that a totalitarian state is the result.

All we have to do is consider the examples of this in our **recent history** of the past 100 years. These are the Union of Soviet Socialists Republic, Nazi Germany, Fascism in Italy, and all of the Communist countries in Eastern Europe, including Romania, Bulgaria, Hungary, Yugoslavia, Czechoslovakia, East Germany, and Poland. Anyone who visited these countries has always noticed how every member of the common society was living under some of the most repressive conditions, and in poverty.

When you look at the men in the leadership of these countries, you always notice that there was always a legacy of people within their own citizenry who were **brutally and often times massively murdered.** Thus there was never any pride of nationalism such that people who understood what was going on were willing to die for the cause. **There was no liberty for which to die, only tyranny!**

## Why Conservatism

George Washington said: "How soon we forget history...Government is not reason. Government is not eloquence. It is force. And, like fire, it is a **dangerous servant** and a **fearful master.**"[65]

---

[65] http://www.great-

As I pointed out in the chapter on Conservatism, the founders of the Constitution wanted the Government as small as possible. The framers of the constitution came together to form a federal government **out of necessity**. During this time, the nation was **already in an undeclared war** with Great Britain. They had to form a federal government in order to give it broad powers that could not apply to the individual states. Thus, it was **never the intention** of the framers of the constitution to create a government to be any larger than what it had to be. Remember that it was because they **each had a vested interest in their individual states** and how they would be affected. They did not want to grant any more broad powers than necessary to an entity which would effectively control these states!

Thus, they created a republic instead of a democracy. As I stated earlier, a republic would give equality to each of the individual states and in so doing; it would automatically limit the power of the federal government. The framers were much more interested in their individual states and the laws that they had already created being maintained well past the necessity of the Continental Congress.

---

quotes.com/quotes/author/George/Washington/pg/2

So when speaking of conservatism, there is one very important fact I would like to state once again, and that is this: **True Conservatism does NOT have an underlying ideology.**

True conservatism only means that it wants to conserve something. In this case, conservatives want to conserve the constitution as it was written almost two and a half centuries ago. This includes the **values** of the framers. That is why many conservatives are Christians. With all of this said, and since we have proven that God does exist, the only conclusion that we can come to is that if we want to preserve the values that this country was founded on, we must be conservatives.

When a President puts his hand on the Bible and repeats the oath of office he states the following:

> "I do solemnly swear (or affirm) that I will faithfully execute the Office of President of the United States, and will to the best of my ability, **preserve, protect and defend** the Constitution of the United States."

It is my contention that if the duly elected President who holds the values of Progressive Liberalism repeats this oath of office with his hand on the Bible, then he has already told **his first lie before God and the nation**. How can I say that? Because the values of Progressive liberalism have an **absolute agenda to radically change the constitution**! This means they do NOT want to preserve it. It means they do not want to protect it. It means they do not want to defend it. In order to repeat the oath of Office as stated **requires** that the duly elected President **hold to conservative values.**

It must be remembered that the Progressive Liberal agenda is to move to a more and more socialistic society. This is a destruction of the Constitution in the following ways:

1. Create a bigger Federal government diminishing the power of the States. This would include modification of sections of the constitution that favors state's rights and elimination of an electoral college.
2. Diminish the power of free market Capitalism, increasing dependence on Government and increasing regulations.
3. Increase taxation to support a bigger government.
4. Schools operated by the Federal Government with history taught in idealistic terms.
5. Radically change the first amendment to restrict Freedom of Speech, and regulate the Press.

6.  Remove gun ownership from the masses.

In fact, I believe that the Liberals would like to tear up the constitution and re-write it. There are just too many ways in which the Liberal ideology opposes its various sections including the Bill of Rights. If anyone does not believe that this will result in totalitarianism in the long run, then they are showing their ignorance of World History.

## A Time for Action

Throughout the pages of this book, I have tried to outline ideas that we can do to stop the madness that is going on in this country. Now as I conclude, I would like to call to your attention another way that **you can directly help this situation**, and it is a way that is found within the Constitution itself. The founding fathers anticipated that there would come a time when those in power would form an aristocracy of sorts and this would lead to the very abuses of power we now see. Thus in anticipation of this, they put in the Constitution a "back door" so to speak, which allows the states to put a stop to the abuses of power.

Article V of the Constitution deals with abuses of power by giving the states the power to put a stop to them. Under the provisions of this amendment the states have been given the power to call a convention of States during which **they can propose amendments to the Constitution**. Then the states themselves can ratify these amendments, thereby bypassing completely both houses of Congress.

That is why I would **implore you** to go to the website **www.conventionofstates.com,** and **sign the petition for your state** to call for the convention of States as allowed by the Constitution. This website outlines four abuses of power that are in dire need of correction. However, in my opinion, there is one more abuse of power that must be rectified, and I will mention this first.

We must call for an amendment to deal with the issue of **term limits** on the House of Representatives and the Senate. Why is this necessary? Because our Representatives and Senators have made the **perpetuation** of their political careers **the number one priority** of their jobs. This had led to serious abuses of power. Why do you think that these elitists become so rich by the time they leave office? This is true on both sides of the political aisle.

The other four abuses of power, as mentioned on the Convention of states website mentioned above are as listed below. I have highlighted and elaborated on **the most shocking aspects** of these issues. There is a link below to this information, as listed on the website.

## 1. The Spending and Debt Crisis

The number one problem in our nation for our children to face is the staggering **$20 trillion national debt**, but if you think this is the extent of our debt, you are wrong. Under standard accounting practices, the federal government **owes around $100 trillion more** in vested Social Security benefits and other programs. This is why the government cannot tax its way out of debt. **Even if it confiscated everything**, it would not cover the debt.

## 2. The Regulatory Crisis

The federal bureaucracy has placed a regulatory burden upon businesses that is complex, conflicted, and crushing. This has caused two serious issues for businesses; starting a business, and staying in business. Little accountability exists when agencies—rather than Congress—enact the real substance of the law. Research from the American Enterprise Institute shows that since 1949, federal regulations have lowered the real GDP growth by 2% and made America **72% poorer**.

## 3. Congressional Attacks on State Sovereignty

For years, Congress has been **using federal grants to keep the states under its control.** But where does the money come for such grants? You guessed it - nowhere! Combining these grants with federal mandates, Congress has turned state legislatures into their regional agencies rather than respecting them as truly independent governments of our Republic, as intended by the Founding Fathers, giving them too much control over the States. This Social program is an invasion of the rights of the people in these states. While significant efforts have been made to combat this social erosion, these trends defy some of the most important principles intended by the Founding Fathers.

## 4. Federal Takeover of the Decision-Making Process

As we stated in the beginning of this book, the Founders believed that the structures of a limited government would provide the greatest protection of liberty. They were interested in making sure that the individual states would not be impeded by the federal government. Not only were there to be checks and balances between the branches of the federal government, power was to be shared **between the states and federal government,** with the latter only exercising those powers specifically granted in the Constitution. However, it is clear that collusion among decision-makers in Washington, D.C., has replaced these checks and balances. The federal judiciary supports Congress and the White House in their ever-escalating attack upon the jurisdiction of the fifty states.

**Note: Although I elaborated on them, I did not write this list.** You can find it on the website below.[66] I would like to once again **urge you** to go to this website, and sign the petition. By taking this action, you will be taking the first steps to help us reclaim our Republic! Remember that the reason our government was created was out of necessity, due to the oppression of the British throne, and the burdensome regulations placed on the people. Because the founders highly valued their individual states, they made our government to be a Republic with shared powers. The federal government has been in the process of trying to remove this power for years. This is not a partisan issue. The elitists in Washington D.C. will never relinquish this power on their own. **It is up to us. This means you!** Thank God we have Article V

---

[66] https://www.conventionofstates.com/problem

of the constitution. No matter which side of the aisle you are on, Democrat or Republican, help us take back our Republic, and sign the petition.

## Conclusion

The Constitution was purposely written to bind the government from totalitarianism by limiting the power of the individual branches. The old saying that "power corrupts and absolute power absolutely corrupts" has been shown by history to be true. John Adams stated: "It is weakness rather than wickedness which renders men unfit to be trusted with unlimited power."[67]

It is because we have the Constitution that we can keep from having a government of tyranny. In the pages of this book we find solutions. But these solutions are bound up in the conservation of the ideals within this precious document. There has been a trend in recent years to ignore many things written in it, and for liberal judges to legislate from the bench. What we do is important. We must do our part to roll up our sleeves and see to it that the constitution is the fully functioning law of the Federal Government as written while not

---

[67]

http://thinkexist.com/quotation/it_is_weakness_rather_than_wickedness_which/183556.html trampling on state's rights. This includes active involvement in the political process.

My fellow Americans, I would like to quote President Abraham Lincoln in closing:

> "America will never be destroyed from the outside. If we falter and lose our freedoms, it will be because we destroyed ourselves."

May we dwell on this, pray about it, and take action, in order that this statement will never be true.

# APPENDIX 1

# Email letter to your Congressional Representatives, and Senators:

## RE: Lying in the News Media

Dear Senator _____,
Dear Representative _____,
The mainstream News media is lying to the American People in a way that is **unprecedented** in the history of this country. In fact it has become apparent that the News media has become a **propaganda Arm** for the Liberal agenda. While I realize that the First Amendment allows freedom of speech in this country, it is an atrocity for the mainstream News media to lie to the American people as they have been doing, and should be considered as hate speech. We who elected you are asking that you demand an investigation into this, complete with public hearings to shame them into stopping this atrocious behavior. Please know that I am available to discuss this with you.

Signed,
Name
Address
City, State, Zip
Phone Number
(Note: This letter is meant to be a model. Please Personalize this letter.)

# APPENDIX 2

# The Declaration of Independence

*IN CONGRESS, JULY 4, 1776*
*The Unanimous Declaration of the thirteen United*
*States of America*

When in the Course of human events it becomes necessary
for one people to dissolve the political bands which have
connected them with another and to assume among the
powers of the earth, the separate and equal station to which
the Laws of Nature and of Nature's God entitle them, a
decent respect to the opinions of mankind requires that they
should declare the causes which impel them to the
separation.
We hold these truths to be self-evident, that all men are
created equal, that they are endowed by their Creator with
certain unalienable Rights, that among these are Life, Liberty
and the pursuit of Happiness. — That to secure these rights,
Governments are instituted among Men, deriving their just
powers from the consent of the governed, — That whenever
any Form of Government becomes destructive of these ends,
it is the Right of the People to alter or to abolish it, and to
institute new Government, laying its foundation on such
principles and organizing its powers in such form, as to them
shall seem most likely to effect their Safety and Happiness.
Prudence, indeed, will dictate that Governments long
established should not be changed for light and transient
causes; and accordingly all experience hath shewn that
mankind are more disposed to suffer, while evils are
sufferable than to right themselves by abolishing the forms
to which they are accustomed. But when a long train of

abuses and usurpations, pursuing invariably the same Object evinces a design to reduce them under absolute Despotism, it is their right, it is their duty, to throw off such Government, and to provide new Guards for their future security. — Such has been the patient sufferance of these Colonies; and such is now the necessity which constrains them to alter their former Systems of Government. The history of the present King of Great Britain is a history of repeated injuries and usurpations, all having in direct object the establishment of an absolute Tyranny over these States. To prove this, let Facts be submitted to a candid world.

He has refused his Assent to Laws, the most wholesome and necessary for the public good.

He has forbidden his Governors to pass Laws of immediate and pressing importance, unless suspended in their operation till his Assent should be obtained; and when so suspended, he has utterly neglected to attend to them.

He has refused to pass other Laws for the accommodation of large districts of people, unless those people would relinquish the right of Representation in the Legislature, a right inestimable to them and formidable to tyrants only.

He has called together legislative bodies at places unusual, uncomfortable, and distant from the depository of their Public Records, for the sole purpose of fatiguing them into compliance with his measures.

He has dissolved Representative Houses repeatedly, for opposing with manly firmness his invasions on the rights of the people.

He has refused for a long time, after such dissolutions, to cause others to be elected, whereby the Legislative Powers, incapable of Annihilation, have returned to the People at large for their exercise; the State remaining in the mean time exposed to all the dangers of invasion from without, and convulsions within.

He has endeavoured to prevent the population of these States; for that purpose obstructing the Laws for Naturalization of Foreigners; refusing to pass others to encourage their migrations hither, and raising the conditions of new Appropriations of Lands.

He has obstructed the Administration of Justice by refusing his Assent to Laws for establishing Judiciary Powers.

He has made Judges dependent on his Will alone for the tenure of their offices, and the amount and payment of their salaries.

He has erected a multitude of New Offices, and sent hither swarms of Officers to harass our people and eat out their substance.

He has kept among us, in times of peace, Standing Armies without the Consent of our legislatures.
He has affected to render the Military independent of and superior to the Civil Power.

He has combined with others to subject us to a jurisdiction foreign to our constitution, and unacknowledged by our laws; giving his Assent to their Acts of pretended Legislation:
For quartering large bodies of armed troops among us:
For protecting them, by a mock Trial from punishment for any Murders which they should commit on the Inhabitants of these States:
For cutting off our Trade with all parts of the world:
For imposing Taxes on us without our Consent:
For depriving us in many cases, of the benefit of Trial by Jury:
For transporting us beyond Seas to be tried for pretended offences:
For abolishing the free System of English Laws in a neighbouring Province, establishing therein an Arbitrary government, and enlarging its Boundaries so as to render it at once an example and fit instrument for introducing the same absolute rule into these Colonies

For taking away our Charters, abolishing our most valuable Laws and altering fundamentally the Forms of our Governments:
For suspending our own Legislatures, and declaring themselves invested with power to legislate for us in all cases whatsoever.

He has abdicated Government here, by declaring us out of his Protection and waging War against us.

He has plundered our seas, ravaged our coasts, burnt our towns, and destroyed the lives of our people.

He is at this time transporting large Armies of foreign Mercenaries to compleat the works of death, desolation, and tyranny, already begun with circumstances of Cruelty & Perfidy scarcely paralleled in the most barbarous ages, and totally unworthy the Head of a civilized nation.

He has constrained our fellow Citizens taken Captive on the high Seas to bear Arms against their Country, to become the executioners of their friends and Brethren, or to fall themselves by their Hands.

He has excited domestic insurrections amongst us, and has endeavoured to bring on the inhabitants of our frontiers, the merciless Indian Savages whose known rule of warfare, is an undistinguished destruction of all ages, sexes and conditions.

In every stage of these Oppressions We have Petitioned for Redress in the most humble terms: Our repeated Petitions have been answered only by repeated injury. A Prince, whose character is thus marked by every act which may define a Tyrant, is unfit to be the ruler of a free people.

Nor have We been wanting in attentions to our British brethren. We have warned them from time to time of attempts by their legislature to extend an unwarrantable jurisdiction over us. We have reminded them of the circumstances of our emigration and settlement here. We have appealed to their native justice and magnanimity, and we have conjured them by the ties of our common kindred to disavow these usurpations, which would inevitably interrupt our connections and correspondence. They too have been deaf to the voice of justice and of consanguinity. We must, therefore, acquiesce in the necessity, which denounces our Separation, and hold them, as we hold the rest of mankind, Enemies in War, in Peace Friends.

We, therefore, the Representatives of the united States of America, in General Congress, Assembled, appealing to the Supreme Judge of the world for the rectitude of our intentions, do, in the Name, and by Authority of the good People of these Colonies, solemnly publish and declare, That these united Colonies are, and of Right ought to be Free and Independent States, that they are Absolved from all Allegiance to the British Crown, and that all political connection between them and the State of Great Britain, is and ought to be totally dissolved; and that as Free and Independent States, they have full Power to levy War, conclude Peace, contract Alliances, establish Commerce, and to do all other Acts and Things which Independent States may of right do. — And for the support of this Declaration, with a firm reliance on the protection of Divine Providence, we mutually pledge to each other our Lives, our Fortunes, and our sacred Honor.

New Hampshire:
Josiah Bartlett, William Whipple, Matthew Thornton
Massachusetts:
John Hancock, Samuel Adams, John Adams, Robert Treat Paine, Elbridge Gerry
Rhode Island:
Stephen Hopkins, William Ellery
Connecticut:
Roger Sherman, Samuel Huntington, William Williams, Oliver Wolcott
New York:
William Floyd, Philip Livingston, Francis Lewis, Lewis Morris
New Jersey:

Richard Stockton, John Witherspoon, Francis Hopkinson, John Hart, Abraham Clark
Pennsylvania:
Robert Morris, Benjamin Rush, Benjamin Franklin, John Morton, George Clymer, James Smith, George Taylor, James Wilson, George Ross
Delaware:
Caesar Rodney, George Read, Thomas McKean
Maryland:
Samuel Chase, William Paca, Thomas Stone, Charles Carroll of Carrollton
Virginia:
George Wythe, Richard Henry Lee, Thomas Jefferson, Benjamin Harrison, Thomas Nelson, Jr., Francis Lightfoot Lee, Carter Braxton
North Carolina:
William Hooper, Joseph Hewes, John Penn
South Carolina:
Edward Rutledge, Thomas Heyward, Jr., Thomas Lynch, Jr., Arthur Middleton
Georgia:
Button Gwinnett, Lyman Hall, George Walton

*This document can be found at:*
*http://www.ushistory.org/Declaration/document/*

# APPENDIX 3

# The Constitution of the United States

Preamble

We the People of the United States, in Order to form a more perfect Union, establish Justice, insure domestic Tranquility, provide for the common defence, promote the general Welfare, and secure the Blessings of Liberty to ourselves and our Posterity, do ordain and establish this Constitution for the United States of America.

### Article. I. - The Legislative Branch

Section 1 - The Legislature

All legislative Powers herein granted shall be vested in a Congress of the United States, which shall consist of a Senate and House of Representatives.

Section 2 - The House

The House of Representatives shall be composed of Members chosen every second Year by the People of the several States, and the Electors in each State shall have the

Qualifications requisite for Electors of the most numerous Branch of the State Legislature.

No Person shall be a Representative who shall not have attained to the Age of twenty five Years, and been seven Years a Citizen of the United States, and who shall not, when elected, be an Inhabitant of that State in which he shall be chosen.

(Representatives and direct Taxes shall be apportioned among the several States which may be included within this Union, according to their respective Numbers, which shall be determined by adding to the whole Number of free Persons, including those bound to Service for a Term of Years, and excluding Indians not taxed, three fifths of all other Persons.) (The previous sentence in parentheses was modified by the 14th Amendment, section 2.) The actual Enumeration shall be made within three Years after the first Meeting of the Congress of the United States, and within every subsequent Term of ten Years, in such Manner as they shall by Law direct. The Number of Representatives shall not exceed one for every thirty Thousand, but each State shall have at Least one Representative; and until such enumeration shall be made, the State of New Hampshire shall be entitled to chuse three, Massachusetts eight, Rhode Island and Providence Plantations one, Connecticut five, New York six, New Jersey four, Pennsylvania eight, Delaware one, Maryland six, Virginia ten, North Carolina five, South Carolina five and Georgia three.

When vacancies happen in the Representation from any State, the Executive Authority thereof shall issue Writs of Election to fill such Vacancies.

The House of Representatives shall chuse their Speaker and other Officers; and shall have the sole Power of Impeachment.

Section 3 - The Senate

The Senate of the United States shall be composed of two Senators from each State, (chosen by the Legislature thereof,) (The preceding words in parentheses superseded by 17th Amendment, section 1.) for six Years; and each Senator shall have one Vote.

Immediately after they shall be assembled in Consequence of the first Election, they shall be divided as equally as may be into three Classes. The Seats of the Senators of the first Class shall be vacated at the Expiration of the second Year, of the second Class at the Expiration of the fourth Year, and of the third Class at the Expiration of the sixth Year, so that one third may be chosen every second Year; (and if Vacancies happen by Resignation, or otherwise, during the Recess of the Legislature of any State, the Executive thereof may make temporary Appointments until the next Meeting of the Legislature, which shall then fill such Vacancies.) (The preceding words in parentheses were superseded by the 17th Amendment, section 2.)

No person shall be a Senator who shall not have attained to the Age of thirty Years, and been nine Years a Citizen of the United States, and who shall not, when elected, be an Inhabitant of that State for which he shall be chosen.

The Vice President of the United States shall be President of the Senate, but shall have no Vote, unless they be equally divided.

The Senate shall chuse their other Officers, and also a President pro tempore, in the absence of the Vice President, or when he shall exercise the Office of President of the United States.

The Senate shall have the sole Power to try all Impeachments. When sitting for that Purpose, they shall be on Oath or Affirmation. When the President of the United States is tried, the Chief Justice shall preside: And no Person shall be convicted without the Concurrence of two thirds of the Members present.

Judgment in Cases of Impeachment shall not extend further than to removal from Office, and disqualification to hold and enjoy any Office of honor, Trust or Profit under the United States: but the Party convicted shall nevertheless be liable and subject to Indictment, Trial, Judgment and Punishment, according to Law.

Section 4 - Elections, Meetings

The Times, Places and Manner of holding Elections for Senators and Representatives, shall be prescribed in each State by the Legislature thereof; but the Congress may at any time by Law make or alter such Regulations, except as to the Place of Chusing Senators.

The Congress shall assemble at least once in every Year, and such Meeting shall (be on the first Monday in December,) (The preceding words in parentheses were superseded by the 20th Amendment, section 2.) unless they shall by Law appoint a different Day.

Section 5 - Membership, Rules, Journals, Adjournment

Each House shall be the Judge of the Elections, Returns and Qualifications of its own Members, and a Majority of each shall constitute a Quorum to do Business; but a smaller number may adjourn from day to day, and may be authorized to compel the Attendance of absent Members, in such Manner, and under such Penalties as each House may provide.

Each House may determine the Rules of its Proceedings, punish its Members for disorderly Behavior, and, with the Concurrence of two-thirds, expel a Member.

Each House shall keep a Journal of its Proceedings, and from time to time publish the same, excepting such Parts as may in their Judgment require Secrecy; and the Yeas and Nays of the Members of either House on any question shall, at the Desire of one fifth of those Present, be entered on the Journal.

Neither House, during the Session of Congress, shall, without the Consent of the other, adjourn for more than three days, nor to any other Place than that in which the two Houses shall be sitting.

Section 6 - Compensation

(The Senators and Representatives shall receive a Compensation for their Services, to be ascertained by Law, and paid out of the Treasury of the United States.) (The preceding words in parentheses were modified by the 27th Amendment.) They shall in all Cases, except Treason, Felony and Breach of the Peace, be privileged from Arrest during their Attendance at the Session of their respective Houses, and in going to and returning from the same; and for any Speech or Debate in either House, they shall not be questioned in any other Place.

No Senator or Representative shall, during the Time for which he was elected, be appointed to any civil Office under the Authority of the United States which shall have been created, or the Emoluments whereof shall have been increased during such time; and no Person holding any Office under the United States, shall be a Member of either House during his Continuance in Office.

Section 7 - Revenue Bills, Legislative Process, Presidential Veto

All bills for raising Revenue shall originate in the House of Representatives; but the Senate may propose or concur with Amendments as on other Bills.

Every Bill which shall have passed the House of Representatives and the Senate, shall, before it become a Law, be presented to the President of the United States; If he approve he shall sign it, but if not he shall return it, with his Objections to that House in which it shall have originated, who shall enter the Objections at large on their Journal, and proceed to reconsider it. If after such Reconsideration two thirds of that House shall agree to pass the Bill, it shall be sent, together with the Objections, to the other House, by which it shall likewise be reconsidered, and if approved by two thirds of that House, it shall become a Law. But in all such Cases the Votes of both Houses shall be determined by Yeas and Nays, and the Names of the Persons voting for and against the Bill shall be entered on the Journal of each House respectively. If any Bill shall not be returned by the President within ten Days (Sundays excepted) after it shall have been presented to him, the Same shall be a Law, in like Manner as if he had signed it, unless the Congress by their Adjournment prevent its Return, in which Case it shall not be a Law.

Every Order, Resolution, or Vote to which the Concurrence of the Senate and House of Representatives may be necessary (except on a question of Adjournment) shall be presented to the President of the United States; and before the Same shall take Effect, shall be approved by him, or being disapproved by him, shall be repassed by two thirds of the Senate and House of Representatives, according to the Rules and Limitations prescribed in the Case of a Bill.

Section 8 - Powers of Congress

The Congress shall have Power To lay and collect Taxes, Duties, Imposts and Excises, to pay the Debts and provide for the common Defence and general Welfare of the United States; but all Duties, Imposts and Excises shall be uniform throughout the United States;

To borrow money on the credit of the United States;

To regulate Commerce with foreign Nations, and among the several States, and with the Indian Tribes;

To establish an uniform Rule of Naturalization, and uniform Laws on the subject of Bankruptcies throughout the United States;

To coin Money, regulate the Value thereof, and of foreign Coin, and fix the Standard of Weights and Measures;

To provide for the Punishment of counterfeiting the Securities and current Coin of the United States;

To establish Post Offices and Post Roads;

To promote the Progress of Science and useful Arts, by securing for limited Times to Authors and Inventors the exclusive Right to their respective Writings and Discoveries;

To constitute Tribunals inferior to the supreme Court;

To define and punish Piracies and Felonies committed on the high Seas, and Offenses against the Law of Nations;

To declare War, grant Letters of Marque and Reprisal, and make Rules concerning Captures on Land and Water;

To raise and support Armies, but no Appropriation of Money to that Use shall be for a longer Term than two Years;

To provide and maintain a Navy;

To make Rules for the Government and Regulation of the land and naval Forces;

To provide for calling forth the Militia to execute the Laws of the Union, suppress Insurrections and repel Invasions;

To provide for organizing, arming, and disciplining the Militia, and for governing such Part of them as may be employed in the Service of the United States, reserving to the States respectively, the Appointment of the Officers, and the Authority of training the Militia according to the discipline prescribed by Congress;

To exercise exclusive Legislation in all Cases whatsoever, over such District (not exceeding ten Miles square) as may, by Cession of particular States, and the acceptance of Congress, become the Seat of the Government of the United States, and to exercise like Authority over all Places purchased by the Consent of the Legislature of the State in which the Same shall be, for the Erection of Forts, Magazines, Arsenals, dock-Yards, and other needful Buildings; And

To make all Laws which shall be necessary and proper for carrying into Execution the foregoing Powers, and all other Powers vested by this Constitution in the Government of the United States, or in any Department or Officer thereof.

Section 9 - Limits on Congress

The Migration or Importation of such Persons as any of the States now existing shall think proper to admit, shall not be prohibited by the Congress prior to the Year one thousand eight hundred and eight, but a tax or duty may be imposed on such Importation, not exceeding ten dollars for each Person.

The privilege of the Writ of Habeas Corpus shall not be suspended, unless when in Cases of Rebellion or Invasion the public Safety may require it.

No Bill of Attainder or ex post facto Law shall be passed.

(No capitation, or other direct, Tax shall be laid, unless in Proportion to the Census or Enumeration herein before directed to be taken.) (Section in parentheses clarified by the 16th Amendment.)

No Tax or Duty shall be laid on Articles exported from any State.

No Preference shall be given by any Regulation of Commerce or Revenue to the Ports of one State over those of another: nor shall Vessels bound to, or from, one State, be obliged to enter, clear, or pay Duties in another.

No Money shall be drawn from the Treasury, but in Consequence of Appropriations made by Law; and a regular Statement and Account of the Receipts and Expenditures of all public Money shall be published from time to time.

No Title of Nobility shall be granted by the United States: And no Person holding any Office of Profit or Trust under them, shall, without the Consent of the Congress, accept of any present, Emolument, Office, or Title, of any kind whatever, from any King, Prince or foreign State.

Section 10 - Powers prohibited of States

No State shall enter into any Treaty, Alliance, or Confederation; grant Letters of Marque and Reprisal; coin Money; emit Bills of Credit; make any Thing but gold and silver Coin a Tender in Payment of Debts; pass any Bill of Attainder, ex post facto Law, or Law impairing the Obligation of Contracts, or grant any Title of Nobility.

No State shall, without the Consent of the Congress, lay any Imposts or Duties on Imports or Exports, except what may be absolutely necessary for executing it's inspection Laws: and the net Produce of all Duties and Imposts, laid by any State on Imports or Exports, shall be for the Use of the Treasury of the United States; and all such Laws shall be subject to the Revision and Controul of the Congress.

No State shall, without the Consent of Congress, lay any duty of Tonnage, keep Troops, or Ships of War in time of Peace, enter into any Agreement or Compact with another State, or with a foreign Power, or engage in War, unless actually invaded, or in such imminent Danger as will not admit of delay.

## Article. II. - The Executive Branch

Section 1 - The President

The executive Power shall be vested in a President of the United States of America. He shall hold his Office during the Term of four Years, and, together with the Vice-President chosen for the same Term, be elected, as follows:

Each State shall appoint, in such Manner as the Legislature thereof may direct, a Number of Electors, equal to the whole

Number of Senators and Representatives to which the State may be entitled in the Congress: but no Senator or Representative, or Person holding an Office of Trust or Profit under the United States, shall be appointed an Elector.

(The Electors shall meet in their respective States, and vote by Ballot for two persons, of whom one at least shall not lie an Inhabitant of the same State with themselves. And they shall make a List of all the Persons voted for, and of the Number of Votes for each; which List they shall sign and certify, and transmit sealed to the Seat of the Government of the United States, directed to the President of the Senate. The President of the Senate shall, in the Presence of the Senate and House of Representatives, open all the Certificates, and the Votes shall then be counted. The Person having the greatest Number of Votes shall be the President, if such Number be a Majority of the whole Number of Electors appointed; and if there be more than one who have such Majority, and have an equal Number of Votes, then the House of Representatives shall immediately chuse by Ballot one of them for President; and if no Person have a Majority, then from the five highest on the List the said House shall in like Manner chuse the President. But in chusing the President, the Votes shall be taken by States, the Representation from each State having one Vote; a quorum for this Purpose shall consist of a Member or Members from two-thirds of the States, and a Majority of all the States shall be necessary to a Choice. In every Case, after the Choice of the President, the Person having the greatest Number of Votes of the Electors shall be the Vice President. But if there should remain two or more who have equal Votes, the Senate shall chuse from them by Ballot the Vice-President.) (This clause in parentheses was superseded by the 12th Amendment.)

The Congress may determine the Time of chusing the Electors, and the Day on which they shall give their Votes; which Day shall be the same throughout the United States.

No person except a natural born Citizen, or a Citizen of the United States, at the time of the Adoption of this Constitution, shall be eligible to the Office of President; neither shall any Person be eligible to that Office who shall not have attained to the Age of thirty-five Years, and been fourteen Years a Resident within the United States.

(In Case of the Removal of the President from Office, or of his Death, Resignation, or Inability to discharge the Powers and Duties of the said Office, the same shall devolve on the Vice President, and the Congress may by Law provide for the Case of Removal, Death, Resignation or Inability, both of the President and Vice President, declaring what Officer shall then act as President, and such Officer shall act accordingly, until the Disability be removed, or a President shall be elected.) (This clause in parentheses has been modified by the 20th and 25th Amendments.)

The President shall, at stated Times, receive for his Services, a Compensation, which shall neither be increased nor diminished during the Period for which he shall have been elected, and he shall not receive within that Period any other Emolument from the United States, or any of them.

Before he enter on the Execution of his Office, he shall take the following Oath or Affirmation:

"I do solemnly swear (or affirm) that I will faithfully execute the Office of President of the United States, and will to the best of my Ability, preserve, protect and defend the Constitution of the United States."

Section 2 - Civilian Power over Military, Cabinet, Pardon Power, Appointments

The President shall be Commander in Chief of the Army and Navy of the United States, and of the Militia of the several States, when called into the actual Service of the United States; he may require the Opinion, in writing, of the principal Officer in each of the executive Departments, upon any subject relating to the Duties of their respective Offices, and he shall have Power to Grant Reprieves and Pardons for Offenses against the United States, except in Cases of Impeachment.

He shall have Power, by and with the Advice and Consent of the Senate, to make Treaties, provided two thirds of the Senators present concur; and he shall nominate, and by and with the Advice and Consent of the Senate, shall appoint Ambassadors, other public Ministers and Consuls, Judges of the supreme Court, and all other Officers of the United States, whose Appointments are not herein otherwise provided for, and which shall be established by Law: but the Congress may by Law vest the Appointment of such inferior Officers, as they think proper, in the President alone, in the Courts of Law, or in the Heads of Departments.

The President shall have Power to fill up all Vacancies that may happen during the Recess of the Senate, by granting Commissions which shall expire at the End of their next Session.

Section 3 - State of the Union, Convening Congress

He shall from time to time give to the Congress Information of the State of the Union, and recommend to their Consideration such Measures as he shall judge necessary and expedient; he may, on extraordinary Occasions, convene both Houses, or either of them, and in Case of Disagreement between them, with Respect to the Time of Adjournment, he may adjourn them to such Time as he shall think proper; he shall receive Ambassadors and other public Ministers; he shall take Care that the Laws be faithfully executed, and shall Commission all the Officers of the United States.

Section 4 - Disqualification

The President, Vice President and all civil Officers of the United States, shall be removed from Office on Impeachment for, and Conviction of, Treason, Bribery, or other high Crimes and Misdemeanors.

## Article III. - The Judicial Branch

Section 1 - Judicial powers

The judicial Power of the United States, shall be vested in one supreme Court, and in such inferior Courts as the Congress may from time to time ordain and establish. The Judges, both of the supreme and inferior Courts, shall hold their Offices during good Behavior, and shall, at stated Times, receive for their Services a Compensation which shall not be diminished during their Continuance in Office.

Section 2 - Trial by Jury, Original Jurisdiction, Jury Trials

(The judicial Power shall extend to all Cases, in Law and Equity, arising under this Constitution, the Laws of the United States, and Treaties made, or which shall be made, under their Authority; to all Cases affecting Ambassadors, other public Ministers and Consuls; to all Cases of admiralty and maritime Jurisdiction; to Controversies to which the United States shall be a Party; to Controversies between two or more States; between a State and Citizens of another State; between Citizens of different States; between Citizens of the same State claiming Lands under Grants of different

States, and between a State, or the Citizens thereof, and foreign States, Citizens or Subjects.) (This section in parentheses is modified by the 11th Amendment.)

In all Cases affecting Ambassadors, other public Ministers and Consuls, and those in which a State shall be Party, the supreme Court shall have original Jurisdiction. In all the other Cases before mentioned, the supreme Court shall have appellate Jurisdiction, both as to Law and Fact, with such Exceptions, and under such Regulations as the Congress shall make.

The Trial of all Crimes, except in Cases of Impeachment, shall be by Jury; and such Trial shall be held in the State where the said Crimes shall have been committed; but when not committed within any State, the Trial shall be at such Place or Places as the Congress may by Law have directed.

Section 3 - Treason

Treason against the United States, shall consist only in levying War against them, or in adhering to their Enemies, giving them Aid and Comfort. No Person shall be convicted of Treason unless on the Testimony of two Witnesses to the same overt Act, or on Confession in open Court.

The Congress shall have power to declare the Punishment of Treason, but no Attainder of Treason shall work Corruption of Blood, or Forfeiture except during the Life of the Person attainted.

## Article. IV. - The States

Section 1 - Each State to Honor all others

Full Faith and Credit shall be given in each State to the public Acts, Records, and judicial Proceedings of every other

State. And the Congress may by general Laws prescribe the Manner in which such Acts, Records and Proceedings shall be proved, and the Effect thereof.

Section 2 - State citizens, Extradition

The Citizens of each State shall be entitled to all Privileges and Immunities of Citizens in the several States.

A Person charged in any State with Treason, Felony, or other Crime, who shall flee from Justice, and be found in another State, shall on demand of the executive Authority of the State from which he fled, be delivered up, to be removed to the State having Jurisdiction of the Crime.

(No Person held to Service or Labour in one State, under the Laws thereof, escaping into another, shall, in Consequence of any Law or Regulation therein, be discharged from such Service or Labour, But shall be delivered up on Claim of the Party to whom such Service or Labour may be due.) (This clause in parentheses is superseded by the 13th Amendment.)

Section 3 - New States

New States may be admitted by the Congress into this Union; but no new States shall be formed or erected within the Jurisdiction of any other State; nor any State be formed by the Junction of two or more States, or parts of States, without the Consent of the Legislatures of the States concerned as well as of the Congress.

The Congress shall have Power to dispose of and make all needful Rules and Regulations respecting the Territory or other Property belonging to the United States; and nothing in this Constitution shall be so construed as to Prejudice any Claims of the United States, or of any particular State.

Section 4 - Republican government

The United States shall guarantee to every State in this Union a Republican Form of Government, and shall protect each of them against Invasion; and on Application of the Legislature, or of the Executive (when the Legislature cannot be convened) against domestic Violence.

## Article. V. - Amendment

The Congress, whenever two thirds of both Houses shall deem it necessary, shall propose Amendments to this Constitution, or, on the Application of the Legislatures of two thirds of the several States, shall call a Convention for proposing Amendments, which, in either Case, shall be valid to all Intents and Purposes, as part of this Constitution, when ratified by the Legislatures of three fourths of the several States, or by Conventions in three fourths thereof, as the one or the other Mode of Ratification may be proposed by the Congress; Provided that no Amendment which may be made prior to the Year One thousand eight hundred and eight shall in any Manner affect the first and fourth Clauses in the Ninth Section of the first Article; and that no State, without its Consent, shall be deprived of its equal Suffrage in the Senate.

## Article. VI. - Debts, Supremacy, Oaths

All Debts contracted and Engagements entered into, before the Adoption of this Constitution, shall be as valid against the United States under this Constitution, as under the Confederation.

This Constitution, and the Laws of the United States which shall be made in Pursuance thereof; and all Treaties made, or which shall be made, under the Authority of the United States, shall be the supreme Law of the Land; and the Judges in every State shall be bound thereby, any Thing in the Constitution or Laws of any State to the Contrary notwithstanding.

The Senators and Representatives before mentioned, and the Members of the several State Legislatures, and all executive and judicial Officers, both of the United States and of the several States, shall be bound by Oath or Affirmation, to support this Constitution; but no religious Test shall ever be required as a Qualification to any Office or public Trust under the United States.

## Article. VII. - Ratification

The Ratification of the Conventions of nine States, shall be sufficient for the Establishment of this Constitution between the States so ratifying the Same.

Done in Convention by the Unanimous Consent of the States present the Seventeenth Day of September in the Year of our Lord one thousand seven hundred and Eighty seven and of the Independence of the United States of America the Twelfth. In Witness whereof We have hereunto subscribed our Names.

Go Washington - President and deputy from Virginia

New Hampshire - John Langdon, Nicholas Gilman

Massachusetts - Nathaniel Gorham, Rufus King

Connecticut - Wm Saml Johnson, Roger Sherman

New York - Alexander Hamilton

New Jersey - Wil Livingston, David Brearley, Wm Paterson, Jona. Dayton

Pensylvania - B Franklin, Thomas Mifflin, Robt Morris, Geo. Clymer, Thos FitzSimons, Jared Ingersoll, James Wilson, Gouv Morris

Delaware - Geo. Read, Gunning Bedford jun, John Dickinson, Richard Bassett, Jaco. Broom

Maryland - James McHenry, Dan of St Tho Jenifer, Danl Carroll

Virginia - John Blair, James Madison Jr.

North Carolina - Wm Blount, Richd Dobbs Spaight, Hu Williamson

South Carolina - J. Rutledge, Charles Cotesworth Pinckney, Charles Pinckney, Pierce Butler

Georgia - William Few, Abr Baldwin

Attest: William Jackson, Secretary

The Amendments

**The following are the Amendments to the Constitution.**

**The first ten Amendments collectively are commonly known as:**

**The Bill of Rights.**

**Amendment 1 - Freedom of Religion, Press, Expression. Ratified 12/15/1791.**

Congress shall make no law respecting an establishment of religion, or prohibiting the free exercise thereof; or abridging the freedom of speech, or of the press; or the right of the people peaceably to assemble, and to petition the Government for a redress of grievances.

## Amendment 2 - Right to Bear Arms. Ratified 12/15/1791.

A well regulated Militia, being necessary to the security of a free State, the right of the people to keep and bear Arms, shall not be infringed.

## Amendment 3 - Quartering of Soldiers. Ratified 12/15/1791.

No Soldier shall, in time of peace be quartered in any house, without the consent of the Owner, nor in time of war, but in a manner to be prescribed by law.

## Amendment 4 - Search and Seizure. Ratified 12/15/1791.

The right of the people to be secure in their persons, houses, papers, and effects, against unreasonable searches and seizures, shall not be violated, and no Warrants shall issue, but upon probable cause, supported by Oath or affirmation, and particularly describing the place to be searched, and the persons or things to be seized.

## Amendment 5 - Trial and Punishment, Compensation for Takings. Ratified 12/15/1791.

No person shall be held to answer for a capital, or otherwise infamous crime, unless on a presentment or indictment of a Grand Jury, except in cases arising in the land or naval forces, or in the Militia, when in actual service in time of War or public danger; nor shall any person be subject for the same offense to be twice put in jeopardy of life or limb; nor shall be compelled in any criminal case to be a witness against himself, nor be deprived of life, liberty, or property, without due process of law; nor shall private property be taken for public use, without just compensation.

## Amendment 6 - Right to Speedy Trial, Confrontation of Witnesses. Ratified 12/15/1791.

In all criminal prosecutions, the accused shall enjoy the right to a speedy and public trial, by an impartial jury of the State and district wherein the crime shall have been committed, which district shall have been previously ascertained by law, and to be informed of the nature and cause of the accusation; to be confronted with the witnesses

against him; to have compulsory process for obtaining witnesses in his favor, and to have the Assistance of Counsel for his defence.

## Amendment 7 - Trial by Jury in Civil Cases. Ratified 12/15/1791.

In Suits at common law, where the value in controversy shall exceed twenty dollars, the right of trial by jury shall be preserved, and no fact tried by a jury, shall be otherwise reexamined in any Court of the United States, than according to the rules of the common law.

## Amendment 8 - Cruel and Unusual Punishment. Ratified 12/15/1791.

Excessive bail shall not be required, nor excessive fines imposed, nor cruel and unusual punishments inflicted.

## Amendment 9 - Construction of Constitution. Ratified 12/15/1791.

The enumeration in the Constitution, of certain rights, shall not be construed to deny or disparage others retained by the people.

## Amendment 10 - Powers of the States and People. Ratified 12/15/1791.

The powers not delegated to the United States by the Constitution, nor prohibited by it to the States, are reserved to the States respectively, or to the people.

## Amendment 11 - Judicial Limits. Ratified 2/7/1795.

The Judicial power of the United States shall not be construed to extend to any suit in law or equity, commenced or prosecuted against one of the United States by Citizens of another State, or by Citizens or Subjects of any Foreign State.

## Amendment 12 - Choosing the President, Vice-President. Ratified 6/15/1804.

The Electors shall meet in their respective states, and vote by ballot for President and Vice-President, one of whom, at least, shall not be an inhabitant of the same state with themselves; they shall name in their ballots the person voted for as President, and in distinct ballots the person voted for as Vice-President, and they shall make distinct lists of all persons voted for as President, and of all persons voted for as Vice-President and of the number of votes for each, which lists they shall sign and certify, and transmit sealed to the seat of the government of the United States, directed to the President of the Senate;

The President of the Senate shall, in the presence of the Senate and House of Representatives, open all the certificates and the votes shall then be counted;

The person having the greatest Number of votes for President, shall be the President, if such number be a majority of the whole number of Electors appointed; and if no person have such majority, then from the persons having the highest numbers not exceeding three on the list of those voted for as President, the House of Representatives shall choose immediately, by ballot, the President. But in choosing the President, the votes shall be taken by states, the representation from each state having one vote; a quorum for this purpose shall consist of a member or members from two-thirds of the states, and a majority of all the states shall be necessary to a choice. And if the House of Representatives shall not choose a President whenever the right of choice shall devolve upon them, before the fourth day of March next following, then the Vice-President shall act as President, as in the case of the death or other constitutional disability of the President.

The person having the greatest number of votes as Vice-President, shall be the VicePresident, if such number be a majority of the whole number of Electors appointed, and if no person have a majority, then from the two highest numbers on the list, the Senate shall choose the Vice-President; a quorum for the purpose shall consist of two-thirds of the whole number of Senators, and a majority of the whole number shall be necessary to a choice. But no person constitutionally ineligible to the office of President shall be eligible to that of Vice-President of the United States.

## Amendment 13 - Slavery Abolished. Ratified 12/6/1865.

1. Neither slavery nor involuntary servitude, except as a punishment for crime whereof the party shall have been duly convicted, shall exist within the United States, or any place subject to their jurisdiction.

2. Congress shall have power to enforce this article by appropriate legislation.

## Amendment 14 - Citizenship Rights. Ratified 7/9/1868.

1. All persons born or naturalized in the United States, and subject to the jurisdiction thereof, are citizens of the United States and of the State wherein they reside. No State shall make or enforce any law which shall abridge the privileges or immunities of citizens of the United States; nor shall any State deprive any person of life, liberty, or property, without due process of law; nor deny to any person within its jurisdiction the equal protection of the laws.

2. Representatives shall be apportioned among the several States according to their respective numbers, counting the whole number of persons in each State, excluding Indians not taxed. But when the right to vote at any election for the choice of electors for President and Vice-President of the United States, Representatives in Congress, the Executive and Judicial officers of a State, or the members of the Legislature thereof, is denied to any of the male inhabitants of such State, being twenty-one years of age, and citizens of the United States, or in any way abridged, except for participation in rebellion, or other crime, the basis of representation therein shall be reduced in the proportion which the number of such male citizens shall bear to the

whole number of male citizens twenty-one years of age in such State.

3. No person shall be a Senator or Representative in Congress, or elector of President and Vice-President, or hold any office, civil or military, under the United States, or under any State, who, having previously taken an oath, as a member of Congress, or as an officer of the United States, or as a member of any State legislature, or as an executive or judicial officer of any State, to support the Constitution of the United States, shall have engaged in insurrection or rebellion against the same, or given aid or comfort to the enemies thereof. But Congress may by a vote of two-thirds of each House, remove such disability.

4. The validity of the public debt of the United States, authorized by law, including debts incurred for payment of pensions and bounties for services in suppressing insurrection or rebellion, shall not be questioned. But neither the United States nor any State shall assume or pay any debt or obligation incurred in aid of insurrection or rebellion against the United States, or any claim for the loss or emancipation of any slave; but all such debts, obligations and claims shall be held illegal and void.

5. The Congress shall have power to enforce, by appropriate legislation, the provisions of this article.

## Amendment 15 - Race No Bar to Vote. Ratified 2/3/1870.

1. The right of citizens of the United States to vote shall not be denied or abridged by the United States or by any State on account of race, color, or previous condition of servitude.

2. The Congress shall have power to enforce this article by appropriate legislation.

## Amendment 16 - Status of Income Tax Clarified. Ratified 2/3/1913.

The Congress shall have power to lay and collect taxes on incomes, from whatever source derived, without apportionment among the several States, and without regard to any census or enumeration.

## Amendment 17 - Senators Elected by Popular Vote. Ratified 4/8/1913.

The Senate of the United States shall be composed of two Senators from each State, elected by the people thereof, for six years; and each Senator shall have one vote. The electors in each State shall have the qualifications requisite for electors of the most numerous branch of the State legislatures.

When vacancies happen in the representation of any State in the Senate, the executive authority of such State shall issue writs of election to fill such vacancies: Provided, That the legislature of any State may empower the executive thereof to make temporary appointments until the people fill the vacancies by election as the legislature may direct.

This amendment shall not be so construed as to affect the election or term of any Senator chosen before it becomes valid as part of the Constitution.

## Amendment 18 - Liquor Abolished. Ratified 1/16/1919. Repealed by Amendment 21, 12/5/1933.

1. After one year from the ratification of this article the manufacture, sale, or transportation of intoxicating liquors within, the importation thereof into, or the exportation thereof from the United States and all territory subject to the

jurisdiction thereof for beverage purposes is hereby prohibited.

2. The Congress and the several States shall have concurrent power to enforce this article by appropriate legislation.

3. This article shall be inoperative unless it shall have been ratified as an amendment to the Constitution by the legislatures of the several States, as provided in the Constitution, within seven years from the date of submission hereof to the States by the Congress.

## Amendment 19 - Women's Suffrage. Ratified 8/18/1920.

The right of citizens of the United States to vote shall not be denied or abridged by the United States or by any State on account of sex.

Congress shall have power to enforce this article by appropriate legislation.

## Amendment 20 - Presidential, Congressional Terms. Ratified 1/23/1933.

1. The terms of the President and Vice President shall end at noon on the 20th day of January, and the terms of Senators and Representatives at noon on the 3d day of January, of the years in which such terms would have ended if this article had not been ratified; and the terms of their successors shall then begin.

2. The Congress shall assemble at least once in every year, and such meeting shall begin at noon on the 3d day of January, unless they shall by law appoint a different day.

3. If, at the time fixed for the beginning of the term of the President, the President elect shall have died, the Vice President elect shall become President. If a President shall not have been chosen before the time fixed for the beginning of his term, or if the President elect shall have failed to qualify, then the Vice President elect shall act as President until a President shall have qualified; and the Congress may by law provide for the case wherein neither a President elect nor a Vice President elect shall have qualified, declaring who shall then act as President, or the manner in which one who is to act shall be selected, and such person shall act accordingly until a President or Vice President shall have qualified.

4. The Congress may by law provide for the case of the death of any of the persons from whom the House of Representatives may choose a President whenever the right of choice shall have devolved upon them, and for the case of the death of any of the persons from whom the Senate may choose a Vice President whenever the right of choice shall have devolved upon them.

5. Sections 1 and 2 shall take effect on the 15th day of October following the ratification of this article.

6. This article shall be inoperative unless it shall have been ratified as an amendment to the Constitution by the legislatures of three-fourths of the several States within seven years from the date of its submission.

## Amendment 21 - Amendment 18 Repealed. Ratified 12/5/1933.

1. The eighteenth article of amendment to the Constitution of the United States is hereby repealed.

2. The transportation or importation into any State, Territory, or possession of the United States for delivery or use therein of intoxicating liquors, in violation of the laws thereof, is hereby prohibited.

3. The article shall be inoperative unless it shall have been ratified as an amendment to the Constitution by conventions in the several States, as provided in the Constitution, within seven years from the date of the submission hereof to the States by the Congress.

## Amendment 22 - Presidential Term Limits. Ratified 2/27/1951.

1. No person shall be elected to the office of the President more than twice, and no person who has held the office of President, or acted as President, for more than two years of a term to which some other person was elected President shall be elected to the office of the President more than once. But this Article shall not apply to any person holding the office of President, when this Article was proposed by the Congress, and shall not prevent any person who may be holding the office of President, or acting as President, during the term within which this Article becomes operative from holding the office of President or acting as President during the remainder of such term.

2. This article shall be inoperative unless it shall have been ratified as an amendment to the Constitution by the legislatures of three-fourths of the several States within seven years from the date of its submission to the States by the Congress.

## Amendment 23 - Presidential Vote for District of Columbia. Ratified 3/29/1961.

1. The District constituting the seat of Government of the United States shall appoint in such manner as the Congress may direct: A number of electors of President and Vice President equal to the whole number of Senators and Representatives in Congress to which the District would be entitled if it were a State, but in no event more than the least populous State; they shall be in addition to those appointed by the States, but they shall be considered, for the purposes of the election of President and Vice President, to be electors appointed by a State; and they shall meet in the District and perform such duties as provided by the twelfth article of amendment.

2. The Congress shall have power to enforce this article by appropriate legislation.

## Amendment 24 - Poll Tax Barred. Ratified 1/23/1964.

1. The right of citizens of the United States to vote in any primary or other election for President or Vice President, for electors for President or Vice President, or for Senator or

Representative in Congress, shall not be denied or abridged by the United States or any State by reason of failure to pay any poll tax or other tax.

2. The Congress shall have power to enforce this article by appropriate legislation.

## Amendment 25 - Presidential Disability and Succession. Ratified 2/10/1967.

1. In case of the removal of the President from office or of his death or resignation, the Vice President shall become President.

2. Whenever there is a vacancy in the office of the Vice President, the President shall nominate a Vice President who shall take office upon confirmation by a majority vote of both Houses of Congress.

3. Whenever the President transmits to the President pro tempore of the Senate and the Speaker of the House of Representatives his written declaration that he is unable to discharge the powers and duties of his office, and until he transmits to them a written declaration to the contrary, such powers and duties shall be discharged by the Vice President as Acting President.

4. Whenever the Vice President and a majority of either the principal officers of the executive departments or of such other body as Congress may by law provide, transmit to the President pro tempore of the Senate and the Speaker of the House of Representatives their written declaration that the President is unable to discharge the powers and duties of his office, the Vice President shall immediately assume the powers and duties of the office as Acting President.

Thereafter, when the President transmits to the President pro tempore of the Senate and the Speaker of the House of Representatives his written declaration that no inability exists, he shall resume the powers and duties of his office unless the Vice President and a majority of either the principal officers of the executive department or of such other body as Congress may by law provide, transmit within four days to the President pro tempore of the Senate and the Speaker of the House of Representatives their written declaration that the President is unable to discharge the powers and duties of his office. Thereupon Congress shall decide the issue, assembling within forty eight hours for that purpose if not in session. If the Congress, within twenty one days after receipt of the latter written declaration, or, if Congress is not in session, within twenty one days after Congress is required to assemble, determines by two thirds vote of both Houses that the President is unable to discharge the powers and duties of his office, the Vice President shall continue to discharge the same as Acting President; otherwise, the President shall resume the powers and duties of his office.

## Amendment 26 - Voting Age Set to 18 Years. Ratified 7/1/1971.

1. The right of citizens of the United States, who are eighteen years of age or older, to vote shall not be denied or abridged by the United States or by any State on account of age.

2. The Congress shall have power to enforce this article by appropriate legislation.

## Amendment 27 - Limiting Congressional Pay Increases. Ratified 5/7/1992.

No law, varying the compensation for the services of the Senators and Representatives, shall take effect, until an election of Representatives shall have intervened.

*This file was prepared by USConstitution.net. Find us on the web at http://www.usconstitution.net.*

# ABOUT THE AUTHOR

D. Robert Pike (Rob) is a retired Engineer and husband of his beloved wife Ida. He holds a Bachelor of Science degree from Indiana Wesleyan University, a Master of Arts Degree from Webster University, and Ph.D in Theology at Trinity College and Seminary.

He is the author of three books:

1. **"God's Promise of Redemption, a story of fulfilled prophecy,"**
2. **"God's Purpose for Hell, a compelling probe of God's love for the lost."**
3. **Jehovah's Witnesses, Modern Day Arians or Not**

**All of Rob's Books are available at Amazon.com, or by order at your favorite book store.**

Rob is an active member of Gideon's International and often speaks in various churches giving the Gideon message of the power of God's Word. He lives with his wife of 35 years in Southwest Florida in the winter, and central Indiana in the summer.

His life verse is Proverbs 3:5,6:

> "Trust in the LORD with all your heart, and do not lean on your own understanding. In all your ways acknowledge him, and he will make straight your paths."

Be sure to visit Rob's website at: www.truthinliving.net.
If you have questions concerning this book, send an email to Rob at robpike@truthinliving.net.